32 Days with God's Story

By
Mark R. Etter

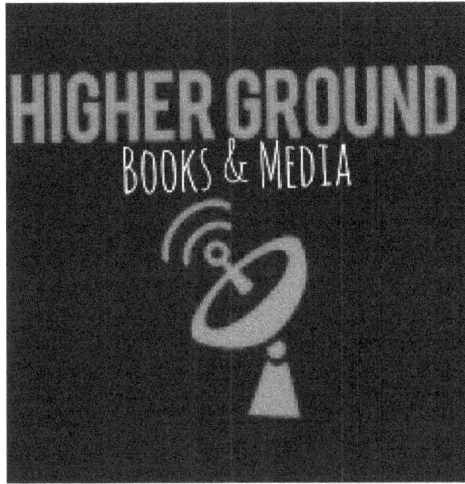

Scripture is taken from the HOLY BIBLE, NEW INTERNATIONAL VERSION®. NIV®. Copyright © 1973, 1978, 1984 by International Bible Society. Used by permission of Zondervan. All rights reserved worldwide.

Higher Ground Books & Media
Springfield, Ohio.
http://highergroundbooksandmedia.com

Printed in the United States of America 2017

The author gives permission for the student Bible studies to be copied for a local church or small group use. A PDF of the student lessons and samples of other books can be found at my website: www.32daysdevotions.com/projects/.

32 Days with God's Story

By
Mark R. Etter

DEDICATION

This book is dedicated to my parents – Roger and Jean who taught me the story of God's love and modeled it for my brothers and me.

Table of Contents

Bible study (by corresponding devotion):
02 Abraham tested - Gen. 22:1-19
03 Joseph Reveals Himself - Gen. 45:1-28
07 The Lord Prepares Joshua - Josh 1:1-18
09 Ruth Meets Boaz - Ruth 2:1-23
11 David Spares Saul - 1 Sam 24:1-22
13 Solomon Asks for Wisdom - 1 Kings 3:1-15
18 Daniel in the Lion's Den - Daniel 6:1-28
20 Mordecai Persuades Esther - Esther 4:1-17
23 Jesus Walks on Water - Matthew 14:22-34
24 Forsaken for You - Matt. 27:32-50
27 Darkness Turns to Joy – Matt: 1-10
29 Paul's Conversion - Acts 9: 1-19

32 days series

This series of devotional books is designed to be a tool that brings you closer to Christ. The devotions are designed to have depth so that you dig below the surface and understand the context. Each devotion is based on a single scripture passage and lays out the events in an organized way to help you comprehend the deeper meanings in the passage and then apply them to your life. As a free gift to you, there are included in this book twelve bible studies that are meant to be shared. You have my permission to copy the student guides for your church or small group bible studies. Each Bible study is connected to one of the devotions and to a leader's guide so that you can feel confident leading others to understand God's word. My hope is that you enjoy these devotions and studies and let the Holy Spirit change your life through them. Read the Bible passage for each devotion and feel free to read the devotions several times as you ponder the message for your life. The twelve bible studies and leader's guides may also lead you to a greater understanding of those texts. God is ready to sit down with you through these devotions and change your life.

Introduction

The Bible is an extraordinary book of ordinary people and a loving God that most people barely know. Let's play a game. Put the following Bible characters in historical order from earliest to latest: A David, B Abraham, C Isaiah, D Paul, E Peter, and F Moses. The correct order is BFACED. If you didn't get them all right, don't feel bad. Many Christians I know can't put them in the exact order either. That is a shame. The Bible is filled with wonderful stories to tell and lessons to teach about each one of those people.

This series of devotions will take you on a ride through much of the history of the Bible with the ups and downs of its people. Around every corner, you will meet individuals who can teach you lessons about how to live a fruitful life or how to avoid destructive habits. You will meet leaders like Joshua and Daniel as well as faithful women like Ruth and Esther. As you get to know them, you will learn lessons that can shape the rest of your life.

Woven in the lives of all these people is the story of a loving God. He will promise extraordinary gifts to some of them. He will teach and mentor these ordinary men and women so that their lives become miraculous. He will even discipline some of them so that they learn how to be great and be a blessing to others. Throughout the ages, the Bible is a diary of God's love for these people and us.

Feel free to work through the devotions over 32 days to get a quick flavor of the Bible in a few weeks. God back if you want and look at the three or four Bible passage sections in each devotion if you want a deeper perspective about that person or era of Bible history. Finally, use the Bible studies at the back to share some of the highlights of your journey with others. Let others have a small sample of what you have learned.

You are on a great adventure. Dig in and learn about the people you will meet one day in heaven. Through the stories of their lives, you will gain new insights into the depth of

God's love for you and the blessings that He wants to give you everyday of your life. May this book be as much of a blessing for you as it has been for me.

1
God Creates a Family
Genesis 2-3
Beginning of time

Context: Before time began, there was only God. The first story of the Bible is a story of love. God created the world as a place where man and woman would live. After furnishing the nursery, He created man and woman so that He might have someone to love.

Imagine the darkest room or a starless night. Imagine a cave so dark that you can't see your fingers and so empty that sound will not carry across the vast space. Into that space, God created a place where His children could live. *"In the beginning, God created the heavens and the earth."* Genesis 1:1 Since God was going to have children; He would have to prepare the nursery. He created light on the first day and separated the up from the down on the second day. On the third day, He made land where people could stand and live. The nursery garden for God's children was empty, and so God took the light and divided it into sun, moon, and stars so that there was time. He filled the water with fish and the sky with birds on the fifth day. Finally, He filled the land with animals so that man had all that he needed to live. And it was good. It wasn't just kind of good. It was perfect.

When God made the man, He made Him different than the animals. *"Then God said, "Let us make man in our image, in our likeness,"* Genesis 1:26 The animals had been called into being but man was shaped by the hand of God out of the dust. Humanity was given the image or quality of God so that he could communicate with God. The man was all alone, so God gave Adam an equal partner. She was created from the rib of man. They were one species and completed each other. God had a purpose for them. They were to care for this world that He had made for them. They were to fill the world with children that God could love. And so, for those first days, Adam and Eve had a love relationship with God.

As a parent, God did not want slaves. He wanted His children to grow and to choose to love Him without force. The Lord had to give them their freedom to love. He had to give them one place where they could decide to disobey. It was a single tree. The angels had already made a choice. Most had chosen to love and obey God. A few, led by one that was called Satan, had decided to rebel. Satan came to earth to lie and make false promises to the woman. She was deceived, and soon man and woman made a choice to disobey God. *"When the woman saw that the fruit of the tree was good for food and pleasing to the eye, and also desirable for gaining wisdom, she took some and ate it." Genesis 3:6.* This simple act of disobedience set in motion the unraveling of a perfect creation.

Birth parents can't stop loving their children, and God was no exception. As we see in the Bible story, God never abandoned man. God loved everyone, even people like Cain and nations like Edom or Moab who would run away from Him. From the very beginning, God promised a Savior to all mankind. He did so because He loved this man and woman whom He created. *"He saved us, not because of righteous things we had done, but because of his mercy. He saved us through the washing of rebirth and renewal by the Holy Spirit," Titus 3:5.* Man's salvation would come in the form of a cross. God would keep that promise because He loved Adam and Eve and God wanted to be with them in eternity. The world wasn't perfect anymore, but it would always be filled with God's love.

The Bible's story with its ups and downs is a love story. A lot of people think that the Bible is a rulebook or a musty history book. As we will see, it is the story of a Father's love as He loves generations of people through the good times and the bad. Those who live in that love are the luckiest people in the world. Because they are God's children, He provides for them and protects them. Because they have a relationship with God, they develop His character and values. They will soar on eagle's wings because they have an edge in this world. They have one they can call Father who will do anything to help them succeed and have real joy.

As you read these devotions, know that the Garden of Eden is still an option. It may not be a place anymore; rather it is a relationship with God. Faith is a little heaven on earth where God loves you, and you can love others. You are free to love others because you live in God's love and are free to be the person that God wanted all men and women to be. The Christian life isn't perfect like the original Eden, but God has a great passion for being with you. He will fill your life with his love. God's love is the greatest gift that you ever will receive. It is the gift that keeps on giving.

· What would life have been like in Eden before the fall? How have you experienced God's love in your life?

2
God Gets Personal
Genesis 12-35
Abraham 2166 – 1991 BC

Context: In the twelfth chapter of Genesis, we see a shift in the Bible's story. The history of mankind in chapter 1-11 becomes the history of Abram and his family. The Old Testament will follow the Jewish people as God gets personally involved with the ones He loves.

A good farmer plays the odds. He plants a whole tray of tomato seeds to make sure that he gets six or eight healthy tomato plants. He cultivates these plants so that together they bring the proper harvest. In the time of the patriarchs, God has a different plan. He throws himself totally into one man. He calls Abram alone from obscurity. There never seems to be a plan B if Abraham fails. God selects Abraham out all the people of the earth and promises to bless him and make a great nation out of him. At chapter twelve, the book of Genesis narrows the focus from God's dealings with the world to God's dealings with Abram and his family. God will nurture them, save them from themselves, and protect them against enormous odds. No other God in history has ever shown such love and devotion. Look carefully, and you will see the depth of God's love for His people and His compassion as He helps His children thrive.

God plants the seed of His love in the dirt of an ordinary man. His promise to Abram is unlike anything that man ever receives in history. It is an unconditional promise from a loving heavenly Father. *"I will make you into a great nation, and I will bless you; I will make your name great, and you will be a blessing." Gen. 12:2* God's promise shows that He has a dream for this man of dirt. He will take this childless man and make him a great nation. These are the dreams that a Father has for His child. Through this man, God will change the world.

Through this man will come the savior of the world and a book of scripture to announce salvation and guide people in life.

God patiently works the soil of this man. Abraham starts to doubt after ten years of waiting. *"But Abram said, "O Sovereign Lord, what can you give me since I remain childless and the one who will inherit my estate is Eliezer of Damascus?" Gen. 15:2* After ten years, Abraham is still a toddler in faith. He does not trust God in a famine, lies about his wife and takes a concubine to accomplish God's "forgotten" promises. Abraham has to grow before the promises can be fulfilled. God will make Abram wait for 25 years before the child will come. During that time, God will teach His child Abram what it means to be a child of God. When God makes a promise, we want it fulfilled now. The wise learn to trust God's timing.

The seedling of a man grows into the stalk of a patriarch. Abraham's relationship grows and deepens so that Lord considers Abraham as He decides the fate of Sodom and Gomorrah. *"The Lord said (to the angels), shall I hide from Abraham what I am about to do?" Genesis 18:17* God decides to use this opportunity to build His friend. Abraham is one of only a few people who know and trust God enough to intercede for others directly with God. He senses that Sodom, where Lot lives, will be destroyed for its evil and struggles with the concept that God would wipe the righteous away with the wicked. The patient dialog helps Abraham understand that there are few righteous people in Sodom. Through the dialog, you see God's love for Abraham and how Abraham cares about others and has learned to trust God intimately.

Every healthy plant needs to be pruned, and so God does the unthinkable at a time when Abraham is almost the man that God desires. Then God said, *"Take your son, your only son, Isaac, whom you love, and go to the region of Moriah. Sacrifice him there as a burnt-offering on one of the mountains I will tell you about." Gen. 22:2* God is pruning His children Abraham and

Isaac of all self-dependence. They will learn to trust God and to obey the Lord no matter how hard life gets. As Abraham and Isaac walk down the hill that day, they have learned a lesson of God's eternal love and commitment to them. It was a painful experience, but some of the greatest lessons are forged in the fire of hardship and pain.

The patriarchs were ordinary people. God came into their lives and fashioned saints from the dirt of ordinary men. God is still willing to work with men and women like you and I. As you look at the patriarchs, watch how God nurtures and prunes people to help them grow. Notice that what makes them extraordinary is that they learned to trust the Lord and follow Him. What we revere is their faith in God. As we follow their descendants throughout the Old Testament, it will be the depth of their faith that will set people apart and provide the blessings that only God can give. Those who trust the Lord will find that God will work day and night to bring His dreams for them to come to pass.

• What goals do you think God has for your life? How much do you trust Him and allow those dreams to become a reality?

3
Put Down the Selfie Stick
Genesis 37-50
Joseph 1915-1805 BC

Context: The descendants of Abraham have grown into a family of 70. Jacob, the grandson of Abraham, has 12 sons. Joseph's story is the account of how one of those sons grew from selfish beginnings to become a leader in a foreign land and save God's people in a time of a great famine.

Athletes have them. Politicians have them. Even high school graduates sometimes have them. They have dreams for the future. It may be to win the World Series or to make lots of money as a doctor. The problem with many of those images is that they are all about the dreamer. Great dreams include others. It is the person who longs to have children to love and mentor. It is the individual who wants to find a cure for cancer or feed the hungry in a third-world country. These are the dreams that are bigger than we are. Joseph's first dreams are self-portraits taken with a selfish "selfie stick." God will transform Joseph's dream into a dream to save the world around him. His life is a lesson in why we need to change our desires into God's vision for us.

The first portrait of Joseph shows the arrogant seventeen-year-old son of Jacob. He is not afraid to snitch on his brothers because he is the all-knowing teenager who thinks he is better than his brothers. His self-centered dreams picture his family bowing down to him as if he is the king. *"Then he had another dream, and he told it to his brothers." Listen,"* he said, *"I had another dream, and this time the sun and moon and eleven stars were bowing down to me." Gen. 37:9* An immature Joseph rubs his brother's faces in this self-portrait rather than wisely keeping the dreams to himself. His pride shows that he is not yet ready to be a leader of the family. His dreams will come true, but only after God has transformed this young man into a humble leader.

The second portrait of Joseph is a prison photo. His selfish dreams have earned his brother's hatred. When visiting his brothers on his father's behalf, Joseph's brothers bind him and sell him as a slave to traders in a caravan bound for Egypt. *"Come, let's sell him to the Ishmaelites and not lay our hands on him; after all, he is our brother, our own flesh and blood." His brothers agreed." Gen. 37:27* So much for the self-proclaimed king. In Egypt, he is falsely accused, thrown into prison and forgotten. His conceit has taken him from prince to prisoner. God is working behind the scenes to prepare Joseph for leadership. His selfish dreams have to be drummed out of him. Thirteen years of hardship will mold him and refine him into a useful tool for the Lord.

The next portrait is one of God's sovereignty. God sends Pharaoh a dream of warning which defies interpretation. Seven sick cows eat seven healthy cows. Finally, someone remembers Joseph. A humble Joseph gives God credit and offers to give God's message to Pharaoh. *"Then Joseph said to Pharaoh, "The dreams of Pharaoh are one and the same. God has revealed to Pharaoh what he is about to do." Gen. 41:25* He tells the Pharaoh that there will be seven bountiful years followed by seven years of famine. God's warning will save the Egyptian people from starvation. Pharaoh senses God's wisdom in Joseph and appoints Joseph to lead the people through the years of famine. Joseph's work will be to carry out God's dream of helping others.

Finally, we see a family portrait. For seven years, the harvest is abundant, but then the years of famine arrive. Jacob sends his sons to Egypt for food. Fifteen years after they last saw Joseph, the brothers bow before him in their quest for food.

On the first visit, Joseph tests his brothers to see if they have changed. On the second visit, Joseph reveals himself and forgives them. Hardship has changed Joseph into a humble servant. *"But God sent me ahead of you to preserve for you a remnant on earth and to save your lives by a great deliverance."* *Gen. 45:7* Joseph has given up his dream in exchange for God's dream. The self-centered boy has become a generous and caring leader. He has become God's tool of deliverance for His people.

Joseph's first dreams were "selfie stick" photos taken at the expense of others. God used hardship to refine Joseph so that the arrogant young man matured into a humble servant and savior of his people. Joseph became God's tool to transform this family into a nation hundreds of thousands strong. God will break into our dreams of self-glory. He may let those dreams crumble and blow like dust in the wind. He replaces selfish goals with a vision of humble service. Those who listen to the Lord can become people whom the Lord can use for greater dreams. Put down your selfie stick so God may give something better. God will make us part of His big picture. Swap your dreams for His, so you can see a brighter picture develop around you.

• What dreams do you have for your life that would make the world a better place? What dreams about yourself may you have to let go if God is going to use you as a tool to change the world?

4
Pharaoh, Let My People Go!
Book of Exodus
The exodus from Egypt 1446 BC

Context: Four hundred years have passed from the time of Joseph. The family of 70 has grown to a great multitude. The guests who were given the best of lands are now slaves to a Pharaoh who fears their numbers but needs their labor.

Life has its good moments and its bad. The perfect job can slowly become a drudgery that we hate. What may start as discomfort can soon become a full-blown coronary. When do you cry out to the Lord for help? How bad does it have to get before you pray about it for five minutes or an hour? Our tendency is to wait too long. We deny that our problems are atrocious and think that they will go away. We don't want to bother the Lord with our troubles even though He is always willing to help. We cause ourselves a lot of pain by not crying out to the Lord. The book of Exodus is the story of a nation crying out and a God who delivered them. God was waiting for Israel to cry out for help, but it took a long time for them to call.

I imagine that the first years in Egypt were golden. Joseph was the second in command, and he gave his family of 70 people the best land in Egypt as their own. Prosperity brings contempt. For four hundred years, the Jews multiplied from a few dozen to hundreds of thousands. Leadership changed in Egypt, and the new leaders began to be afraid of the Israelites and enslaved them. Finally, it got bad enough that God's people thought of God. *"The Lord said, "I have indeed seen the misery of my people in Egypt. I have heard them crying out because of their slave drivers, and I am concerned about their suffering."* *Exodus 3:7* Why does it have to get that bad before people think of God? Why do we wait until we are desperate and need a miracle for things to get better?

How would God save His people from the mighty Egyptians? God had been preparing such a man for 40 years. God saw to it that Moses trained in Egyptian schools and learned the principles of leadership and education. Surely, Moses was ready to lead God's people. Moses threw it all away in a fit of anger when he killed an Egyptian who was beating a fellow Jew. Everything God has worked on for forty years was almost destroyed. Forty years later, God called an eighty-year-old Moses at the burning bush to save God's people. Moses questions the choice. *"But Moses said to God, "Who am I, that I should go to Pharaoh and bring the Israelites out of Egypt?" Exodus 3:11* Yes, Moses is a desert outlaw, but God will bring a miracle through this flawed man.

Amazingly, God sends this man and his brother to face the mighty Pharaoh with a simple demand. "Let my people go". God knew that there would be resistance, but God was sure of the outcome. *"Because of my mighty hand, he will let them go; because of my mighty hand he will drive them out of his country." Exodus 6:1* True to God's word, Pharaoh was stubborn. Each time Pharaoh said no to God, God brought another plague on Egypt. 10 plagues in all were directed at the gods of Egypt like the Sun God Ra and Mother God Isis. God will not be mocked. Those who stand in His way will face His wrath. Those who refuse to listen to God will find their lives face difficulty.

Finally, Pharaoh gets the message when the last plague takes his son, the crown prince. He acts in anger more than faith. *"During the night Pharaoh summoned Moses and Aaron and said, "Up! Leave my people, you and the Israelites!" Exodus 12:31* On their way out of Egypt, the Jews plunder the Egyptians. Gold, Silver, precious fabric and jewels are given them just so that they go away and take their Almighty God with them. The

Jews leave Egypt as a wealthy nation with the possessions needed to build a future. God will lead them to the Promised Land where He wants them to create a nation of faith and live in peace. Everything that God promised to Abraham 600 years earlier is ready to happen. God has a plan for His people.

The good news in this story is the mighty miracle that God worked for His people. The bad news is that they waited 400 years to ask. Their delay put generations in slavery before freedom came. God did more than His people ever hoped or dreamed. The journey of Exodus is a story of new horizons. God not only freed the people from slavery; He led the people into the Promised Land. Where does God want to take you? How bad does it have to get in life before you cry out to the Lord and ask for His plan? God has a wonderful plan for every one of His people. He wants to rewrite your history so that you don't have to live as slaves to this world but can live free as His people. God can take us to places we cannot even imagine.

- How bad does it have to get before you seek God's help? What is keeping you from asking for the future that He wants for you?

5
Creating a Little Heaven on Earth
Exodus 15-40, Leviticus
Mt. Sinai 1445 BC

Context: After a series of ten plagues showing the power of God to the Egyptian Pharaoh, God's people are released from slavery. God's work is unfinished. His people will follow Moses to Mount Sinai so that God can forge a nation out of the former slaves.

Imagine that you live a third world country with no rules and where anarchy reigns. No organization can help you or cares for your needs. There is no recourse if someone steals or kills. Such were lives of the people of Israel as this mob of former slaves assembles and pours out into the desert following Moses. They have no laws and no real leadership as they leave the land of Egypt. The Israelites are now free, but they seem to have no plan, and they are not a nation. How will they become the nation of Israel that God promised Abraham centuries ago? God's answer is to lead them in love to the sacred mountain where He will plant the three seeds needed to build a holy nation. When they arrive at the Promised Land, they will have the tools that they need to build a lasting society under God.

A holy nation needs organization and community. Conflict and troubles develop almost immediately. Long lines form every day as people come to Moses for help and guidance. His father in law Jethro put his finger on the problem. One man can't guide and care for all these people. *"You and these people who come to you will only wear yourselves out. The work is too heavy for you; you cannot handle it alone."* Exodus 18:18 God's first task is to create the structure for a caring community. There will be leaders over thousands, hundreds, and tens. Every person is to be responsible for one another. Every person has someone to care for them. It is the beginning of the modern church working together on common goals for the benefit of all.

A holy nation needs values. At Mt. Sinai, God will define the shape and ideals of the new society. God begins *"You shall have no other gods before me."* Exodus 20:3 Here are the ten pillars of God's vision for a holy nation. The Ten Commandments define the people's relationship with God and each other. The commands give the people a standard to judge what is right and wrong. No longer will man have a fuzzy feeling of values and character. God has spelled out His principles for a joyful life. The Israelites will be a holy people filled with love for each other as they respond to the mercy of God. If the nation lives by these truths, they will live in harmony with one another and will build a healthy and Godly nation.

A holy nation puts God at the center. Camped below the holy mountain, God defines the relationship that He will have with His people. *"Then have them make a sanctuary for me, and I will dwell among them."* Exodus 25:8. In the desert, these people would die without God's help. God will care for them. He will dwell in their midst providing for them and protecting them. They will build a relationship with God so that they depend on Him and can become a holy nation. God will not be distant but will be a daily part of their lives. He will teach His people and guide them so that they slowly have the values and prosperity promised to Abraham long ago. The heavenly Father will mentor His people so that their future can be bright.

God was preparing His people for greatness. He was transforming them from a mob into a nation. We need to think of the Ten Commandments as positive statements for living rather than negative warnings. They summarize God's vision for His people. They encapsulate what it means to be a people of God and how God's children were to live as a holy community. Without these the Ten Commandments and the other two gifts from God, the people of Israel would have died in the desert or returned to slavery. God provided the seeds for real freedom and the nation's future. With God at their center, the caring community was ready to go and claim the Promised Land as their own. They were enabled to become the nation that God envisioned.

Picture what it would be like if we all lived according to the vision God set in the desert. Every man, woman, and child would live with God as the center of their lives. You and I would live without anger and hatred but would take the time to help one another and care for each other's needs. God's love and provision would be everywhere enabling people to live in peace together. It sounds like a fairy tale, but it is a return to God's plan in the Garden of Eden. Such a world is still possible for us. It is the vision that God still has for His people and the impact that they can make on the community around them. His children will thrive and will become a blessing to the world. God still invites all of us to become a holy people by the power of His love.

• What keeps the world from the vision that God has for Israel and the church? How would life according to God's plan improve your future?

6
Follow the Leader
Numbers and Deuteronomy
Wilderness wandering 1446-1406

Context: Leaving Mt. Sinai, the Israelites head north toward
the Promised Land. Instead of trusting the Lord, they rebel
because they fear the people of the land. Their punishment
will be forty years of wandering as their children learn to trust
the Lord.

The Banshee roller coaster at Kings Island sounded like an
excellent idea. The three high school boys laughed and joked
as they waited for a half hour in line. When the trio got to the
front of the line, and Ted saw that his feet would dangle, he
began to have second thoughts. He turned and got out of line.
He was afraid, even though tens of thousands of people safely
rode this ride each year. As Israel wanders in the desert, the
nation must follow the Lord to the Promised Land. This story
is about their disbelief. It is what happens when we try to tell
the Lord what to do instead of trusting the Lord.

The journey from Mt. Sinai started well. God led the
twelve tribes from the holy mountain with a cloud by day and
a pillar of fire by night. "*They set out from the mountain of the
Lord and traveled for three days. The ark of the covenant of the Lord
went before them during those three days to find them a place to
rest.*" Numbers 10:33 As many as a million people walked
together from the mountain up to the land that the Lord had
promised over six hundred years before. Peace lasted only a
few days. The Israelites started complaining about the food
and water. God had worked miracles to bring freedom to His
people only to watch the people enslave themselves in
rebellion.

As they came to the edge of the Promised Land, they
doubted God. They asked to send spies into the land to

confirm God's promises. The spies bring back an evil report and the people rebel. *"Why is the Lord bringing us to this land only to let us fall by the sword? Our wives and children will be taken as plunder. Wouldn't it be better for us to go back to Egypt?"* Numbers 14:3 A whole generation will wander for forty years and die in the desert as the nation learns to trust God. It will take God that long to teach their children to trust Him and prepare them so that they can conquer the Promised Land. It is the price that is too often paid when people question God instead of following Him.

Almost forty years later, the people are still complaining. Faced with a shortage of water, Moses falls face down before the Lord. Now it is his turn to disobey. Frustrated and angry, Moses strikes the rock instead of speaking as God commanded. He must be wondering, "How long will I have to put up with these people and their complaints?" The Lord answers that question. *"But the Lord said to Moses and Aaron, 'Because you did not trust in me enough to honor me as holy in the sight of the Israelites, you will not bring this community into the land I give them."* Numbers 20:12 When God leads, even leaders need to obey.

As the people finally march north to the edge of the Promised Land, there are still questions. "How will we conquer the people of these nations?" God's answer is simple. *"The Lord said to Moses, 'Do not be afraid of him, for I have handed him over to you, with his whole army and his land.."* Numbers 21:34 Victory comes with trust. The enemy is strong, but God is stronger than all our enemies. When the people enter the Promised Land, they will watch the nations fall before the power of our God.

Having success in life is all a matter of trust. None of the Israelite people had ever been outside of Egypt other than Moses. Moses had never been to the Promised Land. They didn't know where to go, but God did. To get to the Promised Land, they needed to follow the Lord. No one in our world knows what the future will hold. We don't have a clue what will be the best course for us for the next five, ten, or twenty years. Those who try to chart their own path will be like people lost and wandering through the desert. Those who seek the Lord and follow Him will find that they have a guide in the wilderness of life. To succeed, we just have to trust God and follow Him.

The Christian faith is not just about getting to heaven. It is also about following God and living with His values in life. God loves you and, like the Jews in the text, He has a path charted for your life. He will walk beside you and lead all who will listen to Him into the life that He has prepared for them. We could wander by ourselves for a lifetime and never find the path. As a Father, He loves you and wants to make your life the best it can be. The question is whether you are willing to let Him lead you through His word or just wander through the wilderness on your own? It is all a matter of trust.

·   How much do you trust God with your future? How are you listening to His desire for your life? Where do you think that God wants to lead you?

7
Do We Dare?
Book of Joshua
Joshua enters Canaan 1406

Context: After forty years of wandering in the desert, Moses dies. On the edge of the Promised Land, Joshua is called by God to lead the people. Will they trust God or will they rebel as they did forty years before?

It was a leadership vacuum. For forty years, the people have followed Moses. Now he is dead just as they are ready to enter the Promised Land. Giants are still in the land as they were forty years before. How will Israel defeat the enemy they were so afraid of? As the story begins, you wonder if this generation will fail as their parents did. God has a different ending in mind. He will encourage this generation and help them to trust Him so that they receive the promise that their parents missed. The book of Joshua is the story of God building His leader and the people so that they can do the impossible. He will lead them into success and show us the path to God's dreams.

God begins with a leader who needs courage. Joshua had waited for Moses at the foot of Mt. Sinai and had been one of the two spies who encouraged the people to follow the Lord forty years before. One senses that Joshua wondered if he could fill the shoes of Moses. God overcomes the doubt with a tremendous promise. *"Have I not commanded you? Be strong and courageous. Do not be terrified; do not be discouraged, for the Lord your God will be with you wherever you go." Joshua 1:9* The time had come for God to fulfill the promise made to Abraham. The land laid before them. It was time to follow the Lord and take the opportunity that God was giving.

Next, God builds up the people of Israel. The Jordan River is at flood stage, and there are a million people to get safely across while the enemy is hiding in the hills watching. Only a miracle will do. God commands them to step out in faith and watch Him do the impossible. *"And as soon as the priests who carry the ark of the Lord–the Lord of all the earth–set foot in the Jordan, its waters flowing downstream will be cut off and stand up in a heap." Joshua 3:13* As they had crossed the Red Sea on dry land, they would now cross the Jordan River with their Lord going before them. It was a sign showing them that nothing was impossible for God. God would go before them and bring about what no one thought could be done.

Jericho was a city with a double wall rising above the river. To a semi-nomadic people with crude weapons, it must have seemed impregnable. God showed them the way to conquer the city. *"March around the city once with all the armed men. Do this for six days." Joshua 6:3* The plan was simple, but it made no sense. The people did not question God's plan but followed as the Ark of the Covenant went before them round the city. The walls came down, and God brought a victory to His faithful people. They had learned to trust God and miracles happened. The land would become theirs.

One man, Achan, did not act faithfully but took some of the spoils of Jericho forbidden by God to His people. God let Israel be defeated at the next battle so that the nation would discover Achan's unfaithfulness. *"Achan replied, "It is true! I have sinned against the Lord, the God of Israel. This is what I have done." Joshua 7:20* Achan and his family died for ignoring God's commands. It may seem harsh, but God was weeding out the distrust and selfishness of His people. It was a lesson for all the people of God to follow Him completely. No one is above God's law.

Every church and every Christian has their defining moments. It is the time when we can play it safe or when we trust the Lord and go forward. The difference between those who trust and those who fail is the same today as it was in the day of Joshua. *"Do not let this Book of the Law depart from your mouth; meditate on it day and night, so that you may be careful to do everything written in it. Then you will be prosperous and successful."* Joshua 1:8. Be in the word, and God will build the faith that you need to move forward. Only those who are in the word on a regular basis will follow God no matter how crazy His plan seems to be.

Faith will succeed where fear pulls us down. Forty years ago, the Israelites heard the reports of the spies and backed off in fear. Under Joshua, the people succeeded. They crossed the flooded Jordan, marched around Jericho and took the Promised Land. God had not changed, but the people had. During the forty years, the people had come to know what God could do. They had grown in their faith and were ready to follow the Lord. Opportunities will be placed before us on a regular basis by our God. He will encourage us and prepare us. Those who have faith will succeed. Those who don't trust Him will fail and miss the blessing.

- What opportunities is God placing before you right now? What will you miss if you do not boldly follow where He will lead?

8
Downward Spiral
Book of Judges
Judges rule 1375-1050 BC

Context: Sixty-five years have passed since Israel left Egypt. During this time, Israel has been a confederation of 12 family tribes and not a united nation. As the people alternate between unbelief and faith, they bring disaster upon themselves, and God must save them from their enemies.

Some people are just doomed to repeat their failures again and again. We have all seen people work out, eat better, and lose 25 pounds. Little by little it came back. Now they have to lose the weight all over again. Others struggle with behaviors like getting up early, stopping smoking, or cutting back on television. Doomed to repeat our failures is the theme of the book of Judges. Over this 330 year period, the Israelites fell away from God, were conquered by a neighboring people, and saved by God only to repeat the cycle again. Their lives remind us that you are doomed to repeat your failures if you don't break out of the cycle by faith.

In the days after Joshua, the people forgot the Lord and began to worship the sensuous false gods around them. "*I said to you, 'I am the Lord your God; do not worship the gods of the Amorites, in whose land you live.' But you have not listened to me.*" *Judges 6:10.* During the conquest of the Promised Land under Joshua, the people had shown tremendous faith. Now, their children had forgotten God. God would rescue them from their enemies only to watch them return to their wicked ways a few years later. The people were their own worst enemy. They would not listen to a loving God but sought out the gods of pleasure.

God is faithful even when His people are not. When the people cried out to God, He raised up a man or woman to judge and save His people. One of those men was Gideon who was such a weak choice that even he recognized it. *"But Lord,"* *Gideon asked, "how can I save Israel? My clan is the weakest in Manasseh, and I am the least in my family."* Judges 6:15 God's purpose in picking Gideon was so that people would see that help came by God's power and not that of a great warrior. God will teach and encourage Gideon so that the people can be rescued and so that Israel might return to their Lord.

Surprisingly, 32,000 men respond to Gideon' call to battle a Midian army numbering over 200,000 warriors. It would take a miracle to save God's people. God wants Israel to know that He won the battle and so He makes a startling command. *"The Lord said to Gideon, "With the three hundred men that lapped I will save you and give the Midianites into your hands. Let all the other men go, each to his own place."* Judges 7:7 God shows the nation what can happen if they trust Him. God would throw the mighty army of Midian into such fear that they would kill each other as they ran from the handful in Gideon's army. It was a miracle that demonstrated God's might. For a moment, it seems like the people have turned to God for good.

The cycle of failure began again after the death of Gideon. *"No sooner had Gideon died than the Israelites again prostituted themselves to the Baals."* Judges 8:33 The people forgot what the Lord had done for them and fell back to their old ways. The people of Israel blended into the surrounding nations instead of standing out with God's values and character. The fertility gods offered more sinful pleasures and fewer restraints. The spiral downward continued and Israel missed the opportunity for revival. The nation was doomed to suffer again because of their unfaithfulness.

Which cycle will you choose for your life? The book of Judges is the story of a foolish people destined to repeat their pain. They remember God only long enough to call out in their pain so that He might rescue them. The people then forgot the Lord as soon as the enemy was defeated and returned to their wicked ways. The wise man and woman know that following the Lord in their life is the key to having a healthy nation filled with blessings. The people enjoyed peace from their enemies and good harvests while judges like Deborah or Gideon were still alive. Life was good because God was at the center of their lives. Unfaithfulness, however, brought the return of slavery and pain.

Imagine a different theme for the story of the Judges. What would it have been like if this was a 300 year period in which the people worshiped the Lord under the string of leaders that God provided? Peace would have pervaded the land and harvests would have been plentiful. In our day, troubles have come to America when its people drift from the Lord. Values are confused, and many are struggling. We don't need to let the spiral downward continue. As we each follow the Lord, we make a small change in our world. Those who commit to worshipping the Lord impact our families and our workplaces. We break the cycle in our little world and can change the nation we live in one family at a time.

- Which cycle do you see in our nation today? How would your faithfulness change the people around you? What would it take to have a different cycle in your world?

9
Never Outside God's Love
Book of Ruth
During the time of Judges 1375-1050 BC

Context: Set during the time of the judges, the story of Ruth shows God's compassion for all people. God welcomes people outside the Jewish nation who have faith. Ruth becomes the ancestor of King David and Jesus Christ.

We have all met people like Tina. In her freshman year of college, she was free of her parents and free to make a lot of bad decisions. There were the parties filled with alcohol, and there were wild boyfriends. She was having the time of her life. Then suddenly she was pregnant and the latest boyfriend disappeared. The promise of a great life vanished in an instant. Seeing no place to go but home, she packed her things and hoped Mom and Dad would accept her. Her parents cried, but they embraced her and welcomed her home. Life could be rebuilt with their love. Ruth is the story of a heavenly Father who welcomes a lost family and gives them a future. It shows that our loving Father is always ready to help repair and renew lives.

Our story begins with a famine and a horrible decision. *"In the days when the judges ruled, there was a famine in the land, and a man from Bethlehem in Judah, together with his wife and two sons, went to live for a while in the country of Moab."* Ruth 1:1 Rather than trust God, Elimelech decides to go to a heathen nation with his wife and two children. He goes to a place that does not worship God. He abandons his God and takes pagan women for his two sons. Here was a family that wasn't just going to live for a little while in this pagan land, but was settling in and making it their home. After ten years, the father and his two sons are all dead. His widow is left with nothing.

God comes to the aid of His people in Judah and ends the

famine. The family in Moab is still struggling. Naomi makes a decision. *"When she heard in Moab that the Lord had come to the aid of his people by providing food for them, Naomi and her daughters-in-law prepared to return home from there."* Ruth 1:6 Those who have left the Lord behind only hear of his blessings, but never experience them. The answer is to repent and return. There would be no blessing for Naomi in Moab. Sadly, Naomi goes home but doesn't get it. Her desire was to go back for food and not for God. She will be in the right place for God's mercy, but she has much to learn about God and sins to confess before real blessings can come her way.

Oddly, it is the pagan daughter Ruth who throws herself on God's mercy. *"And Ruth the Moabitess said to Naomi, "Let me go to the fields and pick up the leftover grain behind anyone in whose eyes I find favor."* Ruth 2:2. Jewish law said that the poor could glean fields already harvested. It was one of God's programs for the feeding of the poor. Ruth took the promise of God at His word and gave God an opportunity to work in her life by living in His law and trusting in His mercy. She was not lazy nor proud. She was hardworking and humble. God was more than ready to act. Help comes when you give God openings to change your life and build your future.

God provides the humble Ruth a husband and a son. *"The women living there said, "Naomi has a son." And they named him Obed. He was the father of Jesse, the father of David."* Ruth 4:17 Naomi who had forgotten God was given an heir who could claim the farmland of Naomi's husband and would provide a future for Naomi and Ruth. We can see God's generosity in that the child would be part of God's plan to change the world. Ruth's son, Obed, would have a grandson named King David and a descendant named Jesus. There is no limit to what God can do if people will live with faith. God can take people whose lives are shattered and lift them to places of honor and great joy. The Lord takes broken lives and brings great joy.

The world is filled with people who feel like they just don't belong. Perhaps you or someone you know feels that way. God has not given up on you. Our God is a loving Father who cares for all His children. The Bible records the stories of many people who seem beyond help. Just a few include the thief on the cross, Saul (St. Paul) who imprisons Christians and even a tax collector named Matthew. Every one of them seems beyond reclamation, but God lifts them all up and changed their lives and their futures. The story of Ruth shows that God can and would like to reclaim them all. Ruth's life changed the moment that she trusted God and was willing to live as a child of God. She went from outsider to becoming an ancestor of Jesus Christ. God wants to keep transforming your life and the lives of the people you love.

• How close are you and your family to the Lord right now? How do you think that is impacting your present and your future? How does the story of Ruth inspire you?

10
Be Different!
1 Samuel 1-15
Saul's Reign 1050-1010 BC

Context: Samuel is the last of the judges. He spoke for the Lord and through his life; he led Israel back to the Lord. In his later years, the people wanted a king like the nations around them and chose Saul as their first king.

Anna passionately wanted to fit into her new school. She wanted to sit at the table with the cool kids at lunch or hang out with them after school, but she knew that would never happen because she was weird. She was a concert pianist who practiced two hours a day. As fate would have it, the accompanist for the school choir broke her arm a week before the big Christmas concert. Anna got up the courage and volunteered to play for the performance. With only two rehearsals, she performed flawlessly and became the talk of the school. Suddenly, it was good to be weird. The story of Samuel and Saul is about a time when God's people just wanted to live like everyone else. They saw themselves as weird and didn't understand how being special was a blessing.

The time of the judges was a time when the people forgot the Lord and became ordinary. Even their leaders had become wicked. *"Now Eli, who was very old, heard about everything his sons were doing to all Israel and how they slept with the women who served at the entrance to the Tent of Meeting."* 1 Sam. 2:22 During the 400 years of the Judges (1 Kings 6:1), the people had forgotten the lessons of the Exodus. They became enslaved by nation after nation. These were very dark days for people who had come out of Egypt and conquered Palestine. Israel had become nothing special at all.

God prepared a leader who would bring His people back to Him. His name was Samuel. People understood that Samuel spoke for God and so, in desperation, the people finally came to Samuel for help against the Philistines. Samuel laid their sins before them and made them put away their false gods and their evil ways. *"If you are returning to the Lord with all your hearts, then rid yourselves of the foreign gods and the Ashtoreths and commit yourselves to the Lord and serve him only, and he will deliver you out of the hand of the Philistines."* 1 Sam. 7:3. God wanted to make His people great again. He would fight for them and make them unique as He was unique.

Under Samuel, the people defeated their enemies and had peace. God was again the Lord of this nation. As Samuel gets old, the people look for a successor. Instead of asking God to raise up another Godly prophet, they seek a worldly solution for their future. *"They said to him, "You are old, and your sons do not walk in your ways; now appoint a king to lead us, such as all the other nations have."* 1 Sam. 8:5 They want a king just like everyone else around them. They want to put their trust in a mighty king and his army instead of trusting the Lord to protect them against all their enemies. They want the palace to be the center of life and not the tabernacle. After years of peace under Samuel, they forget what God alone can do.

God leads them to Saul who looks like the king they desire. Things were good for a while as Saul follows the Lord. There is a danger when men lead. Pride begins to enter Saul, and he begins to think that he doesn't need God. Saul gets impatient and decides to take on battles without the Lord. In the end, the Lord must reject Saul. *"The Lord has sought out a man after his own heart and appointed him leader of his people because you have not kept the Lord's command."* 1 Sam. 13:14 Saul has been leading the people so that they become just like their neighbors. God has in mind a man who will make the tabernacle the center of the nation. Israel will again be different and will defeat its enemies by the power of God.

The stories of Samuel and Saul are a tug between a God who wants His people to be different and people who want to be just like everyone else. The nation of Israel doesn't appreciate what they have when they let the Lord lead. There is a constant struggle when the culture tells us to take the easy way or the way of the crowd. If we want a better life, we have to live differently than the world. We have to let the Lord lead us and protect us.

The world finds God's ways weird, but weird can be wonderful. It is wonderful to have a loving spouse and children with who love to each other and attend church every Sunday. Such a weird life was God's dream for Israel, and it is still His dream for us. Why would you or I want to pay the price of divorce, alcohol, or crushing debt like everyone else? Be weird and follow the Lord so that you can have His blessings and not the life of the crowd. Our God is different, and He gives us the opportunity to be different, too.

- How does your life differ from the world around you? What blessings would come if you were weird and followed God's way more fully in your life?

11
He Had God's Heart
1 Samuel 16 – 2 Samuel 7
Samuel anoints David 1025 BC

Context: Saul was tall and strong, but he soon began to disobey the Lord. The Lord rejected him and chose a young boy from an insignificant family in Bethlehem to be the next king. David stood apart because of his heart for the Lord. He would stand up for God's honor against Goliath, and he would lead his people to worship the Lord.

When we hire someone as our doctor or mechanic, we often consider their skill and knowledge. We want a doctor who has done this procedure dozens of times. We want a mechanic who has worked on this model car with years of experience. They need to get it right. When God looks at a person, he is not impressed with their skill or knowledge. He can give both to any fool. What he cares about is the heart. Is this a person who will follow God and obey Him? When God goes looking for a king to follow Saul and lead His people, He wants a man of character who loves the Lord more than anything else. He finds such a man in David.

When God had rejected Saul for his stubbornness and his unwillingness to repent, God sent Samuel to find the new king in the small village of Bethlehem. After the older sons of Jesse are rejected, God explains His desire. *"Do not consider his appearance or his height, for I have rejected him. The Lord does not look at the things man looks at. Man looks at the outward appearance, but the Lord looks at the heart." 1 Sam. 16:7* Finally, Samuel anoints David. David has the heart to lead the people of God. God will take this shepherd boy and nurture him to be Israel's greatest king. David has God's heart, but what is that exactly?

About a year later, Israel will see David's heart for God. As a teenager, David is still too young to be in the army, but he can deliver food to his older brothers who are fighting the Philistines. Below in the valley, mighty Goliath is shouting curses against the true God. David is incensed that this giant would defile the name of Almighty God. He is willing to fight Goliath for God's honor. He shuns a soldier's armor and faces Goliath defiantly. *"You come against me with sword and spear and javelin, but I come against you in the name of the Lord Almighty, the God of the armies of Israel, whom you have defied." 1 Sam. 17:45.* David will lay his life on the line for God's honor and defeat the giant.

David again shows the heart God is looking for ten years later. King Saul has turned against David, and we find David hiding in the desert. Saul relieves himself in a dark cave where David and his men are hiding. David's men who are tired of running see this as an opportunity from God to kill Saul and have security. David will keep himself pure. *"Some urged me to kill you, but I spared you; I said, 'I will not lift my hand against my master because he is the Lord's anointed.'" 1 Sam. 24:10* The Lord stands behind the righteous and not the evil. David will not kill the Lord's king. How can David expect the Lord to protect him when he becomes king if he is no better than Saul?

Finally, David has now been king for about twenty years, and the Lord has brought David wealth and power. David wants to use this time of peace to build a temple to the Lord so that all the world will honor God and worship Him. *"He (David) said to Nathan the prophet, "Here I am, living in a palace of cedar, while the ark of God remains in a tent." 2 Sam. 7:2* Surprisingly, God says no. It will be Solomon, David's son who will build the temple. God calls David to continue to lead the nation with his example of godliness so that they become a holy nation. Saddened, David accepts the Lord's will. Obedience and submission to the Lord are more important than greatness.

David was a small town shepherd boy with a big heart. He became a great king because he listened to the Lord and because the Lord developed his character and values. Never underestimate the heart. God's people do not need strength or resources; God will provide those. God is looking for people dedicated to Him and open to being His tool in the world. God is looking for men and women with His heart whom He can love and help all the days of their lives. Those who have His heart are the ones that God can use to work in the lives of the community and the nation. God will choose them because their open heart is willing to follow Him and to do His will. The impact such a heart can have is enormous. These are the people we want to have as leaders, coworkers, and friends. They bring God's blessings to everyone that has contact with them. Through them, God can change the world around them because they are willing to follow Him.

- Who do you know that has David's heart for God? What sets them apart from others? What would change in your world if you had that kind of heart?

12
Willing to Repent
2 Samuel
David's reign 1010-970 BC

Context: David committed terrible sins from adultery with Bathsheba to the counting of the "fighting men" of Israel. David, unlike Saul, was always repentant when he sinned and always asked for mercy and forgiveness. The power of the kingship sometimes led him away from God, but his heart always brought him back.

Was David a Godly man? The young David followed the Lord. As we follow David through life, we see a man who seems eviler than the king that he replaced. Saul never committed adultery, murdered a man or allowed his children to rape or kill each other as David did. Why was David honored by God and Saul discarded? On the surface, it doesn't make sense. What David had was not a perfect life, but a humble heart. He sinned but was open to the Lord's rebuke. As you follow David, you see the power of humility before the Lord. No one is without sin, but how you react to sin can make all the difference. David repented when he sinned so that the Lord might forgive and restore him.

Even the best of people fall. David's downfall began on a rooftop. The troops were out at battle, and the middle-aged David was bored and wandering the palace. He sees a beautiful woman and is filled with lust. *"Then David sent messengers to get her. She came to him, and he slept with her." 2 Samuel 11:4.* A one night fling with a lovely woman begins a downfall that will haunt David the rest of his life. To save his neck, he tries to cover up his sin by murdering Bathsheba's husband. David abuses the power that God has given him and soon is adding sin upon sin in a never-ending cover up. Mighty King David has fallen.

A year passes, a baby is born, and it seems like no one has noticed. David thinks he is off the hook, but God will not be mocked. Because His servant has not repented, the Lord sends the prophet Nathan to David. In a simple story, God convicts David of his sin and rebukes him for its destruction upon God's people. *"This is what the Lord says: 'Out of your own household I am going to bring calamity upon you. Before your very eyes I will take your wives and give them to one who is close to you." 2 Sam. 12:11* David's punishment is that his family will fight and cause him great pain. There are consequences for sin.

Psalm 51 gives us an open window into David's heart. He doesn't try to make excuses for what he has done or blame God. He freely admits that he deserves punishment. *"Against you, you only, have I sinned and done what is evil in your sight so that you are proved right when you speak and justified when you judge." Psalm 51:4* David appeals to the Lord's mercy and asks for forgiveness for he knows that he cannot undo what he has done or make it right. He does something most of us never consider. He asks the Lord to make his faith stronger so that he might not sin like this again. His desire is not just to survive the consequences, but to grow in faith and actions.

Here lies the difference between David and Saul. Unlike Saul, David is honest about his sins and their effects. He speaks from the heart about God's mercy when enemies attack or when his character fails. He knows and depends on the Lord. *"As for God, his way is perfect; the word of the Lord is flawless. He is a shield for all who take refuge in him." 2 Sam. 22:31* The Lord was David's refuge and strength in life. He admitted his sin and accepted God's discipline when he was wrong. He clung to the Lord and didn't want to live without the Lord. God was David's bedrock and source of success. David depended on the Lord to keep him on the straight and narrow.

David shows us that God doesn't give up on the repentant sinner. Yes, David was an adulterer and a murderer. The Bible is honest about his flaws, but it also shows the heart of David and his love for the Lord. David shows us that God can still love us when we sin and humbly come before the Lord in repentance. Open up the psalms and feel how sin tears David apart and how David rejoices when God forgives him for his sin. David shows us the path when we stumble. We can reject the Lord and try to make things work like Saul did or we can humbly return to the Lord and confess our sins like David. David had God's heart, a humble heart and it is what separated him from Saul and what made him a great king. When you fall, come back to the Lord so that He can pick you up. His mercy will never let you down. Like David, we can prosper and grow stronger in faith if we bring our sins to the Lord for forgiveness. God never gave up on David, and He will never give up on you if you come to Him to repent.

- When you sin are you more likely to try to defend yourself or throw yourself on God's mercy? As you look at David's life, which works better and why?

13
Laughing, Crying, Cursing, Sighing
Psalms
The Psalms span from Moses (Ps.90) to after the Exile
(Ps.137)

Context: The book of Psalms is often thought of as the Treasury of David with 73 psalms ascribed to him. The Psalms is a hymn book of the ages expressing the emotions and faith of the people of God from the Old Testament up to today.

God created man and woman to have feelings, and they often express those feelings in song. Celebrations are announced with trumpets lifting our hearts. Sadness is often voiced by saxophones playing the blues in a minor key. The ups and downs in the story of life are often expressed in music. It may be for that reason that many Christians claim the psalms as their favorite book. It is real life expressed from the heart. It paints a variety of emotions in such a way that we feel the author's triumph and tragedy with our hearts. Sometimes, the mood is happy as the author praises the Lord for what He has done. Other times, the mood is sad as the author expresses his pain and begs the Lord for help and deliverance. At other times, we find the psalmist cursing their enemies or sighing as they confess their sins. We find them pondering God's work or praising God as a community in worship. The variety among the 150 psalms is incredible. As we understand the moods of the psalms, we can pray with them in worship to our God.

There are times that we want to laugh with God in our prayers. The psalms of thanksgiving express the variety of situations in which our God helps us. We may thank God for His care (Psalm 23), His deliverance (Psalm 30), His forgiveness (Psalm 32) or His kindness (Psalm 118). Sometimes the praise to the Lord details an individual experience. Other times the psalm paints a broad picture of the loving and gracious character of our God. Our hearts reach out and announce to all what God has done. These are psalms help you rejoice and tell everyone what God has done in your life. You can use these psalms to celebrate in your prayers what God has done for you and others.

At times, life has caused us pain and tears streak down our face. Forty-three personal laments and six community laments are scattered across the pages of the Psalms. The laments can be a cry for help (Psalm 70), a longing to be with God (Psalm 42), or a remembrance of God's power in the midst of our pain (Psalm 77). Such psalms often tell the story of a person's pain, express confidence that God can help and ask for God's grace in their time of need. Many of the laments in the Psalms end with praise because the author is confident that the Lord has heard them and that the Lord will help them in their need. These psalms help us when we hurt so that we pray focusing on God and not just our pain.

Sometimes people hurt us so much that we want revenge. The Psalms have a better idea. Six Psalms consider the enemies of Israel to be enemies of God. They ask the Lord to deal with people who have caused them pain. Such psalms may ask for payback when people seek their life (Psalm 35), rule unjustly (Psalm 58), or treated Israel harshly during the captivity (Psalm 137). These psalms may seem harsh when we think of Jesus' appeal to love our enemies (Matt. 5:38-44), but are just a call for God's justice. They ask the Lord to judge and to deal with evil instead of the people of God bringing vengeance. God's people do not want to become as evil as the people who have hurt them. These are psalms you can pray when you have been deeply hurt and seek answers from God.

Finally, every person sins and needs the forgiveness of God. When your sin leaves your heart sighing under the weight of sin, seven psalms can help you approach God. These psalms are built on the bedrock of God's forgiveness and mercy. We can lay our sin before God confident that our

God will forgive us. We may be asking for help when our sins cause us agony (Psalm 6), appeal with King David for cleansing (Psalm 51), or request God for restoration (Psalm 102). The psalmists know the real cost of sin in their relationship with God and their well-being. These psalms can be prayed when life has been shattered by sin.

God's people have sung the Psalms over the ages. The messages have a lyric quality that often rolls off the tongue and echoes the deep yearnings of the heart. I have found that the Psalms have tremendous value in my prayers. As I page through the Psalms, I often find the psalmist expressing feelings that I have deep in my soul. As I speak my emotions in the words of the psalm, the psalmist directs me to new understandings and healing as his faith speaks to mine. I find direction for my prayers as I learn about the nature of my God and His help for my life. More than anywhere else, the Psalms speak to my inner being and bring my soul closer to God.

- What are you feeling right now? Which of the four types of psalms above match your feeling and could help you express your joy or your pain and hurts?

14
Throwing God's Blessings Away
1Kings 1-11, 2 Chron. 1-9
Solomon's reign 970-930 BC

Context: Solomon was the son of David and Bathsheba. He was the richest and wisest man of his day. His kingdom stretched from the border of Egypt to the edge of Assyria. He fell away from the Lord later in life, and his sin split the country in two.

He had it all and threw it all away. We have known people like that. It was the doctor's kid who got into drugs. The brightest kid in the class who got bored and dropped out. Solomon was all that and more. His annual income was 25 tons of gold a year, and he sat on an ivory throne overlaid with gold. God made him the wisest man who ever lived. It should have been a golden era for Israel. It would all disappear in a generation. The kingdom would be torn in two. The riches would evaporate, and Israel would never see peace like that again. Solomon had it all but threw it away. He lusted after women and forgot the true God. Today, we forget how wealthy we are. We live in a time when the danger of throwing it all away as Solomon did is a real possibility.

God had blessed the nation during the time of David. He secured its borders, built a capital city and put His tabernacle at the heart of the empire. God chose Solomon to succeed his father David and offers Solomon anything that Solomon wants. Solomon in his wisdom asks for a discerning heart so that he might rule the people well. God is pleased and offers him even more. *"I will do what you have asked. I will give you a wise and discerning heart, so that there will never have been anyone like you, nor will there ever be."* 1 Kings 3:12. God also will give Solomon riches and honor greater than all the kings of his day. A golden era is ready to begin for Israel. A Godly king will lead them, and God will bless them.

Wise King Solomon took the riches of his father and built a temple in Jerusalem and dedicated it to the Lord. He led the people to honor God and so God appeared to Solomon a second time with a promise. *"As for you, if you walk before me in integrity of heart and uprightness, as David your father did, 'You shall never fail to have a man on the throne of Israel.'"* 1 Kings 9:4-5. Solomon would be the beneficiary of all the promises that the Lord made to David. There was a condition, and that condition was obedience. Solomon needed to be a man like his father. He needed to be one who continued to worship the Lord and lead the people to follow their God. Only a Godly nation could become the beacon of light that God had in mind.

It was lust that took Solomon away. He filled his life with women – 700 wives and 300 concubines from the nations that he conquered. He permitted these women to worship their gods instead of insisting that they worship the Lord. Soon, Solomon changed as well. *"As Solomon grew old, his wives turned his heart after other gods, and his heart was not fully devoted to the Lord his God, as the heart of David his father had been."* 1 Kings 11:4 He loved the women more than he loved God. Soon the nation followed his lead, and God was not the center of the kingdom of Israel. Solomon threw away all God had promised in the pursuit of women.

"Meaningless, Meaningless. . . Everything is meaningless" Ecclesiastes 1:2. He had wealth, power, and wisdom; but it meant nothing. He pursued one pleasure after another, but it only left him empty. Such was life without God. It was a life of having everything, but it gave no joy or delight. America is the land of plenty, but so many are unhappy. So often people seem to have it all but have no satisfaction. We have the wrong priorities. We will stand in line for hours to get a Black Friday bargain, but can't be bothered to come to church. We will spend hours watching sports but complain about listening to a sermon or taking time for Bible study. If the life of Solomon teaches us anything, it is that life without God is

meaningless.

Ecclesiastes also shares Solomon's wise answer to it all. *"Moreover, when God gives any man wealth and possessions and enables him to enjoy them, to accept his lot and be happy in his work--this is a gift of God." Eccl. 5:19* Real joy comes in having a relationship with God and in the knowledge that you and I have a heavenly Father who will keep on giving. Real joy comes in the knowledge that you and I have a heavenly Father who will keep on giving. David built a relationship with God that brought him through his troubles. Those like Solomon who forget the Lord will be doomed to success with little meaning. Enjoy what the Lord has given you and know that He will give more. You can have all the wealth and wisdom in the world, but it will mean nothing without a relationship with God.

- What is one habit that God is calling you to change? How do such habits keep us from the joy that we can have in our Lord?

15
Walk With God or Against Him
1Kings 12-14, 2 Chron. 1-9
The division of the kingdom 930 BC

Context: Rehoboam, the son of Solomon becomes king at his father's death, and his folly splits the kingdom of Israel in two. The northern kingdom will turn its back on God and be lost forever in 722 BC. The Southern Kingdom will alternate between faithful and unfaithful times.

Both powerful and ineffective leaders have changed the course of our nation's history. Washington would be one of the great presidents in almost anyone's book. Buchanan is often rated as one of the worst presidents. He sat and watched the country fall apart in the years before the civil war. As we look at presidents and other leaders, we can see how they are instrumental in the shape of a country. Solomon got the people started on the wrong path, and his successors made things even worse. The constant in the time of the kings was the Lord. God had made promises that the nation would continue and He worked to keep Israel as a nation. He brought the people through this time so that the Messiah could be born among them and could change the world.

Man's folly split the kingdom of David. King Rehoboam is the forty-one-year-old Son of Solomon and grandson of David. As he takes the throne, the people rebel over the high taxes and forced labor imposed by Solomon to support his wealth. Rehoboam makes a fateful decision. *"So the king did not listen to the people, for this turn of events was from the Lord."* 1 *Kings 12:15* Instead of listening to his father's older and wiser counselors, he tells the people that they will have to put up with high taxes. God was punishing the house of David for the worship of false gods in Jerusalem. There are consequences when a leader forgets God and desires wealth and power for himself.

God had given the Northern tribes to a man named Jeroboam. He was an administrator of Solomon's who had fled from his wrath. God had offered to be with Jeroboam if he followed the Lord and worshiped God only. Jeroboam feared that people returning to Jerusalem to worship God would have allegiance to Judah and he created a wicked solution. *"After seeking advice, the king made two golden calves. He said to the people, 'It is too much for you to go up to Jerusalem. Here are your gods, O Israel,"* 1 Kings 12:28 Instead of leading the people toward God, he decided to create false gods so that the people would have allegiance to him and the new nation. Jeroboam took the people of the north away from God. Sadly, they would never come back to the Lord.

Rehoboam, the grandson of David, walked for three years with the Lord like his grandfather David did. When he felt secure, he began to water down worship like his father, Solomon. *"They also set up for themselves high places, sacred stones, and Asherah poles on every high hill and under every spreading tree."* 1 Kings 14:23 The temple was there, but Israel worshiped pagan gods as well. Rehoboam and the people of Judah abandoned God, and so God left them and let Shishak, the king of Egypt, attack the Jews and take away much of Solomon's wealth. God does not allow half way worship. Forgetting God brings consequences for its sinful behavior.

The Northern Kingdom would have nine dynasties rule as king after king would refuse to acknowledge the Lord. In the Southern Kingdom of Judah, David's family would rule for 350 years. Most of the kings of Judah were evil, but some like Asa, Hezekiah and Josiah would lead God's people back to their Lord. In spite of their sins, God was still faithful to David and to the promises that God made to David. Through even the sinful times, God kept a remnant. *"Nevertheless, for David's sake the Lord his God gave him a lamp in Jerusalem by raising up a son to succeed him and by making Jerusalem strong."* 1 Kings 15:4 Even when the church began to forget its God, God would help His people and not let the church be destroyed.

As for each of us, we can either walk with God or against him. Think of one of those moving sidewalks at the airport. If you walk on it the wrong way, you will find yourself constantly struggling. If you travel with it, life becomes easier, and you get to your destination. God is on a march to save people from hell and to bring blessings to those who will follow Him. You can either walk with Him or walk against Him. It is all about how much pain you want to bear in your life. Like a moving sidewalk, the world can go against God for a time, but their foolishness will cause destructive consequences for all who go their way. In the end, whether you walk with God or against Him will determine if your life moves forward or just seems to stand still in one place. Those who go with God's flow will find joy and success as they walk with other Christians. Those who oppose God will be like the fools in the era of the kings who destroyed themselves as they refused to follow the Lord.

- What does a Godly walk look like? What impact has walking with or against God made in your life?

16
Come Home Wayward People
1Kings 1-11, 2 Chron. 1-9
Elijah's ministry 875 -848 BC, Hosea's ministry 750-715 BC

Context: The messages of the sixteen prophets to the northern and southern kingdom are recorded in the Bible. The prophets span from Obadiah in 845 BC to Malachi in 433 BC. Each prophet has a unique message of encouragement and judgment from God.

What would you do if one of your sons suddenly got hooked on drugs and ran away from home? I know that I would track him down and try to reason with him. I would send people I trusted to try to speak to him and convince him to come home because I loved him and I wanted to help. In the days of David and Solomon, Israel had been the envy of the world. It was powerful and had enormous wealth. It showed the greatness of God to the world so that they respected Yahweh. Then Israel ran away from God and worshiped others. God would send prophets to them to demonstrate His power through miracles. The message was always the same. Return to me, and I will restore you. Here is the story of God's heartache with His wayward people.

God tries to lead them back by showing them His power. The great prophet Elijah is called fifty years after the days of Solomon during the rule of the Northern Kingdom's wicked King Ahab. Elijah calls a meeting with Ahab and proposes a challenge between the true God and Ahab's false gods to see who the real God is. 450 prophets of Baal called on their god for hours with no response. Elijah prays to God, and God answers in a way that shows everyone that He alone is the Almighty. *"Then the fire of the Lord fell and burned up the sacrifice, the wood, the stones and the soil, and also licked up the water in the trench."* 1Kings 18:38 On that day, the people cry out that Yahweh is the true God, but sadly their faith doesn't last.

God also tries to lead them back by showing His love. God sends Hosea to the Northern Kingdom 180 years after the days of Solomon. He is to marry a prostitute as a visual message showing how much the Lord loves the nation of Israel which has prostituted itself to the false gods around it. Hosea would love this woman and have children with her, but she would run away. Hosea was commanded to buy his wife out of the slavery of prostitution. *"Go, show your love to your wife again, though she is loved by another and is an adulteress. Love her as the Lord loves the Israelites, though they turn to other gods and love the sacred raisin cakes."* Hosea 3:1 God had not forgotten His people but wanted to reclaim them and have them live in His love.

Because the end is near, God sends a second prophet named Amos to the Northern Kingdom in the days of Hosea. His message is a message of punishment for Israel and Judah. If Hosea shows gospel love, then Amos shows law and justice. Israel is within a generation of being destroyed. It is time to repent before it is too late. His warning seems harsh, but God is pleading with His people to repent. *"Surely the eyes of the Sovereign Lord are on the sinful kingdom. I will destroy it from the face of the earth-- yet I will not totally destroy the house of Jacob,"* declares the Lord." Amos 9:8. The people see no reason to repent. In the end, their rejection of the Lord will bring destruction.

Even as the Northern Kingdom is being destroyed, God sends the prophet Isaiah to the Southern Kingdom with a promise. *"A remnant will return, a remnant of Jacob will return to the Mighty God"* Isaiah 10:21 Israel had left the Lord and Judah ran hot and cold, but God had a message for the faithful. He would not forsake them. The promises that He made to Abraham of a Messiah and a nation as numerous as the stars in the sky had not changed. God looked beyond the destruction of Israel and the Babylonian Captivity of Judah to the day when His people would again follow Him and worship Him. The sovereign Lord will not only judge the wicked, but He will redeem His people and make them great again.

The stories of the prophets are the stories of a God would not give up on His wayward people for over 200 years. It would have been easy to destroy Israel immediately for they never came back to God during the centuries of their existence. God loved them and sent prophets to them with demonstrations of power and a visual demonstration of love. Neither worked. The words of the prophets are still the message of God today. God is calling His people to return to Him so that He might restore them. Our God does not give up on His people. He shows them His power and His love. He is a heavenly father who loves his children even when they are in the midst of sin. It is never too late to cry out to the Lord and seek His mercy and His help. His love never ends and never fails.

• What message do you think the prophets would have for the people in your community? How would things improve if we took the words of the prophets to heart?

17
Watered Down Faith
2 Chronicles 29-33
Hezekiah's reign 715-686 BC

Context: Hezekiah takes the throne of the Southern Kingdom shortly after the fall of the Northern Kingdom. He is a righteous king who is encouraged by Isaiah the prophet. His son, Manasseh is a wicked leader who begins the slide to the Babylonian Captivity

Leaders have the power to change history. Our American presidents have more power than we want to admit. Think of all that Abraham Lincoln gave this country as he saved the union. Think of the disservice that his predecessor, James Buchanan did as he sat by and watched the south secede and did nothing. The times of the Jewish kings were filled with a few good and Godly kings who brought peace and prosperity and a majority of evil kings who worshiped false gods. The contrast can be seen easily in the rules of a father and his son. The Northern Kingdom had been led away from God by evil kings and destroyed in 722 BC. It should have been a warning for the kings of the southern kingdom of Judah to continue to follow the Lord. Hezekiah who took the throne only seven years later did follow the Lord. His son Manasseh led the people away from God and began the fall to the Babylonian captivity.

Hezekiah gave his heart to God. His father Ahaz had been an evil king who worshiped Baal and shut up God's temple. But Hezekiah was different than his father. *"He did what was right in the eyes of the Lord, just as his father David had done. In the first month of the first year of his reign, he opened the doors of the temple of the Lord and repaired them."* 2 Chron. 29:2-3 He began his reign by reclaiming God's temple. He also wanted to claim the hearts of the people, and so he dedicated fourteen men to teach the people about the God that so many of them did not know. He wanted revival in Jerusalem. He wanted the hearts of the nation to be lifted up to the Lord and refused to have empty worship.

When he finds himself in danger, he turns to the Lord. Assyria is on the move and sends its army into Judah demanding surrender. Hezekiah lets his faith shine before the people. *"Hezekiah received the letter from the messengers and read it. Then he went up to the temple of the Lord and spread it out before the Lord."* Isaiah 37:14 In prayer, Hezekiah, and his officers humble themselves before God and seek His protection. God answers by dispatching an "Angel of the Lord" who put to death 185,000 troops camped around the city of Jerusalem in a single night. When God's people pray, great miracles happen. The nation would be spared destruction and would survive for another 100 years after Hezekiah's death.

One would expect that Manasseh would have the faith of Hezekiah, his father. Manasseh would lead Judah away from God. He would rebuild all the false altars that his father had abolished. God sent messengers to warn Manasseh, but the king and the people did not listen to the Lord. The mighty Assyrians came again, and they captured Jerusalem and the king. *"So the Lord brought against them the army commanders of the king of Assyria, who took Manasseh prisoner, put a hook in his nose, bound him with bronze shackles and took him to Babylon."* 2 Chron. 33:11 Manasseh had destroyed the blessings of peace which his father Hezekiah had prayed for at the altar. The downfall of Judah had begun. God will not be mocked.

God didn't give up on Manasseh or the Jewish people. As a captive, Manasseh called out to the true God and was freed by the Lord and brought back to Jerusalem. Manasseh got rid of the foreign gods and cleansed God's temple. The damage was done. *"The people, however, continued to sacrifice at the high places, but only to the Lord their God."* 2 Chron. 33:17 There was confusion among the faithful as they worshiped God at the high places where they had worshiped Baal. The worship of

God had been accommodated to the customs of the surrounding nations. Faith was watered down, and the true nature of God was forgotten. Scripture was lost until the days of his grandson, King Josiah. (2 Chronicles 34:14)

We would do well to continue to pray for our leaders. Good King Hezekiah opened up the temple and the hearts of Judah only to have both closed in the days of his son. Imagine what leaders who are hostile to the Lord could to do America. Churches could be persecuted and shut down as they were in the days of the book of Acts. Evil practices could be legalized and protected, and people would be banned from even criticizing such behavior. The nation would find its enemies overtake them as they did in Manasseh's day and the people would be thrust into war and famine. We must pray and live out our faith so that our nation does not give into the world, but that our country continues to be built around the Lord. God alone is the source of blessing and prosperity for the nation.

- As you think of the current leaders of America, what would you ask of God for them? How have the current leaders been a blessing to the nation? What policies would you ask God to change?

18
Falling on Deaf Ears
2 Chron. 36, Jeremiah and Ezekiel
The fall of Jerusalem 586 BC

Context: The kingdom of Judah had forgotten its God. It may seem harsh, but God would humble His people by allowing a foreign nation to take them captive so that they became dependent on their God.

Jimmy loved to play with fire. His parents would scold him and pull him away from the campfire. As soon as they were not looking, he was back at the fire. More than once, he got burned. How many warnings does it take from God before people start to listen? The last forty-five years of Judah's history were filled with warnings from people like Jeremiah and Ezekiel. No one seemed to take the warnings seriously. They paid the price with seventy years of captivity. Mixed into those warnings was a parent's love. God wasn't just angry with the people of Judah; he was concerned for them. Like any parent whose kids misbehave, God knew that someday his people would get burned. He continued to warn them because He cared that much.

Approximately fifty years before the destruction of Jerusalem, Jeremiah proclaimed a warning to the people of Judah. *"During the reign of King Josiah, the Lord said to me, "Have you seen what faithless Israel has done? She has gone up on every high hill and under every spreading tree and has committed adultery there." Jeremiah 3:6.* Judah had become lukewarm in her faith during the reign of Josiah. The people talked about God but worshiped the gods of the surrounding people. Jeremiah would continue to warn the people through the reign of five kings and three attacks by the Babylonians. He would be arrested, beaten and thrown into a well to die. It would be easier just to keep quiet, but a loving God has to warn people who are sowing the seeds for their destruction.

Jeremiah had warned of the "boiling pot facing north (Jer 1:11), but King Jehoiakim refused to listen. He took Jeremiah's scroll of prophecies and cut it into pieces and burned the pieces. In the fourth year of Jehoiakim's reign, disaster happened. *"During Jehoiakim's reign, Nebuchadnezzar king of Babylon invaded the land, and Jehoiakim became his vassal for three years." 2 Kings 24:1* Babylonia conquered Judah. Daniel and some of the best young men of the kingdom were taken captive and taken to Babylon. It was a warning of the things that were to come if the people did not repent. It should have made them turn to the Lord. The king and the people did not listen even though Jeremiah prophesized that this would begin 70 years of captivity (Jer. 25:12). Often people find themselves suffering, but refuse to turn to the Lord. God weeps because He knows the troubles that will come because of their stubbornness.

Eleven years before the destruction, God soon added another voice of warning when Judah did not listen. After three years under the Babylonians, Jehoiakim successfully rebels against Babylon. Jeremiah warned the people that their lack of repentance would cause their destruction. As God has warned, the Babylonians returned and attacked the nation again. Ezekiel began prophesying to the Jews in Babylon after he and other leaders had been taken in this second wave of conquest. *"I am about to bring a sword against you, and I will destroy your high places." Ezekiel 6:3* Under David, Israel had been a powerful nation; now they were a conquered state with a puppet king and only the lower class left to farm the land. How far does a country or person have to fall before they listen to the Lord?

Finally, the time of warning was over, and destruction would come The Jews had turned to Egypt to save them instead of the Lord, and so the Lord allowed Jerusalem to fall to the Babylonians. *"They set fire to God's temple and broke down the wall of Jerusalem; they burned all the palaces and destroyed everything of value there."* 2 Chron. 36:19 The Babylonians broke the city walls, destroyed the temple and blinded the king. King Zedekiah was led away in chains to Babylon in 586 BC. The Jewish people would be a conquered people. Jeremiah laments the destruction of the city in the book of Lamentations. The powerful nation of David seemed to be gone, but it was God's way of teaching His children how to obey and prosper.

Destruction is not God's final word. The Lord through the prophet Jeremiah had promised that the people would return to the Promised Land 70 years from the time of the first captivity. In Ezekiel, God pledges to bring a revival in the nation of Israel. Not only will he gather them back, but the people who come back will also be forgiven and taught to put away their idols. In common language today, we would call it "tough love." You can talk all you want, but sometimes you have to have tough love. Such is the depth of God's love for His people. Many will not listen to the Lord, but there will always be a remnant who will find the Lord at their side caring for them and loving them no matter how far the nation has fallen. God can't stop loving even when so many don't love Him back.

- Tough love is painful but sometimes necessary. When have you experienced God's tough love? Why can't a loving God just let you do anything you want to do?

19
The Blessings of Obedience
Book of Daniel
Daniel's Ministry 605-536 BC

Context: Daniel is taken in the first conquest of Judah in 605 BC. His dependence on God allows him to rise to leadership while in captivity. He will serve both Babylonian and Persian kings rising to rule over the "whole kingdom" (Daniel 6:3)

One person can make a difference. It had started as a simple Boy Scout camping trip, but things had gone all wrong. The weather turned violent with high winds and blowing snow. The scouts and their leaders panicked, and things looked hopeless. Tom kept his head. He relied on his scout training and built a shelter with a campfire near the van. Others started calming down, and the smoke showed the rescuers where they were. One scout made the difference between life and death. So it was with Daniel. He was taken in the first wave of captives and never gave up his trust in God. He didn't picket or hold protests; He just stood firm in his faith. This man of faith had a significant impact on the people of God and the nation of Babylon.

Daniel was just a teenager taken hundreds of miles from home and family. As a captive in Babylonia, he would learn their language and culture, but he would not break God's food laws. *"But Daniel resolved not to defile himself with the royal food and wine, and he asked the chief official for permission not to defile himself this way."* Dan. 1:8 It didn't matter that he was just a boy taking on an empire. He trusted in God and would not compromise God's law. His actions show why he would become great. God's ways were the best. He stepped forth and led others to obey God no matter what the consequences.

About a year later, King Nebuchadnezzar has a dream. Because he doesn't trust his advisors, he wants them to interpret the dream without revealing the contents to them. Death is the penalty for not understanding the dream correctly. Daniel is also facing death, so he turns to prayer. God reveals the answer to the vision. *"Do not execute the wise men of Babylon. Take me to the king, and I will interpret his dream for him."* Dan. 2:24 As he tells the king what God is saying, Daniel gives all the glory to the Lord. He shows this pagan king that the Hebrew God is the Lord of Lords. What had been a disaster became an opportunity to witness to the majesty of God. The whole kingdom sees the wisdom of God. Daniel is given a high place in the nation because of God's wisdom in his life.

At the age of 80, Daniel's reputation of being trustworthy and loyal has brought him to the highest levels in the kingdom. Those jealous of him want to get rid of him. They have a problem. *"We will never find any basis for charges against this man Daniel unless it has something to do with the law of his God."* Dan. 6:5 They set a trap that will put him in a lion's den because they know He will not refrain from worshipping the true God. Daniel was so devoted to his God that the possibility of death did not keep him from praying. His trust in God is well placed. God will rescue Daniel from the lion's den and demonstrate that He is greater than the gods of the Persians. Daniel's values and faith will have a significant impact on Jew and Gentile alike. The king will glorify the Lord because of Daniel.

In the year Daniel faced the lion's den, Daniel's heart for his people shines brightly. He is praying for the Jewish people and is given an insight from scripture. *"I, Daniel, understood from the Scriptures, according to the word of the Lord given to Jeremiah the prophet that the desolation of Jerusalem would last seventy years."* Dan. 9:2 It had been 70 years since the beginning of captivity. He was too old to return, but he called upon God to show mercy to His people without delay. He admits that the people do not deserve this honor, but calls on God to keep His promise. God listened to Daniel's prayer, and within a short time, a remnant of the Jews would go home to Israel. Daniel was close to the Lord and was not afraid to claim God's promises for his people.

In Daniel, we see the power of one Godly man. At the same time that the Kings of Judah were leading people from God, the teenage Daniel was standing up for the Lord before the king of Babylon. He refused to deny his God, and God used Daniel to bring glory to God's name. Here in this pagan place filled with Babylonian idols, Daniel is a model for us all. God was able to elevate him as a leader and witness to the Jewish people and a series of Babylonian and Persian kings because Daniel put the Lord first. We think that it takes an army to change the world, but Daniel gives a hint at what you or I can do if we have Daniel's values and obedience. God can use us to change the world if we will but follow Him.

• Who do you know who has lived by their Christian values as Daniel did? How do such attitudes and lifestyle lead others to trust and follow such a person in life?

20
Return Home
Ezra 1-6, Haggai 1-2, Zechariah 1, 8
The first exiles return home 538 BC

Context: The first set of exiles returned from Babylon to Palestine in 538. They faced many hardships as they try to resettle Judea. God will send His prophets to encourage the people to put God first and rebuild the temple.

We start but don't finish. How many half-finished projects do you have around the house? Maybe there is a sewing project that was supposed to be done for last Christmas. Maybe there is a yard project that is hoping to be completed next spring or summer. We all have them. We started something and just didn't finish it. Why is it that churches have the same problem? We say that we need to fix the parking lot, but just never get around to it. We say that someone needs to organize Sunday servants, but no one ever does. As the people of God came back from Babylon, They need to rebuild the temple, but the project gets bogged down for fifteen years. God can't fix lives that we don't give him.

The exiles return from Babylon to Judea, and after a short time, they begin to rebuild the altar and the foundations of the temple. The Jews knew that it was important for the Lord to be in their midst if they were going to rebuild their nation and their lives. The neighboring nations did not want God or a rebuilt Jerusalem in their midst. They made it hard for the Jews. *"Thus the work on the house of God in Jerusalem came to a standstill until the second year of the reign of Darius king of Persia."* Ezra 4:24 Rather than fighting for what they thought was important, the people just gave up. They had a letter from King Cyrus that they could build a temple, but they became discouraged and left the temple unfinished.

Fifteen years later, God sends two prophets named Haggai

and Zechariah to the people to admonish them and give them hope. God is tired of waiting and knows that the people will never become the Jewish nation if they don't start putting God first. God chides them for their priorities. *"Is it a time for you yourselves to be living in your paneled houses, while this house remains a ruin?" Haggai 1:4* The people have finished homes that are warm and snug. God's house is still a pile of rubble. The people have made excuses and have gone on with their lives without the Lord. God can wait. There are more important things to do. Life has been hard, and crops have been few. They will never have prosperity without the Lord. It is past time to get busy building God's temple.

What the people have failed to notice is that putting God second or twenty-second in their life has had a negative impact on their lives. *"You have planted much, but have harvested little. You eat but never have enough. You drink but never have your fill. You put on clothes but are not warm. You earn wages, only to put them in a purse with holes in it." Haggai 1:6* They work hard to have a harvest yet they never have enough. They are never warm in their fancy clothes or paneled homes. The prophet reminds them that their priorities are wrong and that they have taken away the great advantage that they should have compared to their neighbors. How can they expect God to bless them when they have put him second place in their lives?

The people listened to Haggai and Zechariah, and the work of the temple began again in earnest. Immediately the workers again faced opposition from the nations around them. They did not stop working but continued to build the temple. They appealed to the Persian authorities, and God's hand was with them. *"But the eye of their God was watching over the elders of the Jews, and they were not stopped until a report could go to Darius and his written reply be received." Ezra 5:5* After four years, God's Temple was rebuilt in Jerusalem, and the people celebrated the dedication of the temple. God was now at the center of the kingdom because the people trusted the Lord to remove the obstacles. Great things do happen when people rely on the Lord. No obstacle can stop our God.

Do we see the value in ministry? The people let the building of the temple slide because it just didn't seem necessary. It was more important for them to have warm homes and fields full of grain than to have a place to worship God. From the earth's perspective, that would make sense. From God's big picture, we see that it is short sighted. I see that the stress people feel and many of the problems they face because God gets put last. They expect Him to fix their lives while they pursue happiness and prosperity outside of God. It doesn't work. God won't fix lives we don't give Him. How many ministries have not been undertaken or have stopped because we didn't think that we had the money or the people to do them? If the church would spend as much time asking God for help and direction as we do in making excuses or in wringing our hands, the church could do the impossible.

• Where have you put God second in your life? How would it make your life smoother and happier if God was first?

21
It is My Problem!
Esther
Esther becomes queen 479 BC

Context: The book of Esther is an example of God's divine guidance and care in the lives of His people. The book of Esther is set about sixty years after the first wave of exiles returns to Jerusalem and about two decades before Ezra returns to Jerusalem.

It is just not my problem! I find myself overwhelmed with the problems of the world each night on the news. It may be an earthquake halfway around the globe or a total stranger who just got cancer. I am overwhelmed because I just can't help them all. You and I wait for someone to take care of the problem. Sometimes that person has to be me! It is our family member with cancer or a friend's home hit by a flood. We may not be able to help everyone, but we need to help someone. Esther is the story of a young woman who must trust God as He uses her to save His people. It reminds us that if everyone else's problems are not my problem, then God can't use us to give His help to the people in need around us.

Sometimes an opportunity comes when you least expect it. Having deposed his wife after he loses an important battle, the lusty king starts looking for new women for his harem. Esther was taken in this sweep of the countryside, but something happened. *"Now the king was attracted to Esther more than to any of the other women, and she won his favor and approval more than any of the other virgins. So he set a royal crown on her head and made her queen instead of Vashti." Esther 2:17* The king was attracted to her. It was not just a one night stand. He made her queen. God watched out for her and turned what could have been a disaster into an opportunity. Esther was now in a position of power and influence.

Soon, friction arises between one of the royal court and Esther's people, the Jews. The evil Haman convinces the king to sign a decree that will begin a slaughter of the Jews. Esther's uncle, Mordecai, brings her the news and he urged her "*to go into the king's presence to beg for mercy and plead with him for her people.*" *Esther 4:8* Esther resists his request because she knows that she will be putting her life on the line. Finally, Esther reluctantly agrees but asks that others join her in three days of fasting and praying. God will protect His people. It is up to us to decide whether we will be part of His team or ignore the Lord and face the consequences.

Only the King could save her people, the Jews. He was the one who had signed the decree, and he was the only one who could help. "*Then Queen Esther answered, "If I have found favor with you, O king, and if it pleases your majesty, grant me my life-- this is my petition. And spare my people--this is my request.*" *Esther 7:3* Making the most of the opportunities is all about courage. It took trust in the Lord to stand up and tell the king that she was a Jew. She told the truth in a caring way and let the king see the real effect of his decree. She knew that keeping quiet and allowing the evil plan to go forward would be the end of her family and, perhaps, of her as well.

Oddly God is never mentioned in the book of Esther, but you can see God's hand on every page. Evil Haman is disgraced and hanged. Esther is rewarded for her courage as the King is moved to help the Jews. Mordecai becomes Prime Minister in Haman's place. It is our caring God meeting the needs of people. The people are still not saved, however. The king must write a new law to counteract Haman's decree. "*The king's edict granted the Jews in every city the right to assemble and protect themselves.*" *Esther 8:11*. The law allows the Jews to turn on the enemy and protect themselves. The annihilation of the Jews never happened. God works behind the scenes in our lives as well doing miracles.

It is all about trusting God enough to act as His tool. When others struggle, it is our problem. We may not be able to help everyone around us, but we need to help some of the people near us. God will work through you. He put you in a place where you have the opportunity to help, and He will provide the resources that you need to do the task because God cares and God wants that person helped. We need to have courage, not because we are a fool, but because we know and believe that God is standing at our side. Imagine if every man thought only of himself, and no one helped anyone else. That would be a miserable place to live. As we help our neighbor and others help us, we will find God working to make our community a better place. We are not in this alone. We go forward as Esther did trusting in the Lord as we help others around us.

• Who do you know who needs a helping hand? What is one thing that you could do to help them today and gain a special friend for the rest of your life?

22
Rebuilding a Nation
Ezra, Nehemiah, and Malachi
Ezra returns 458 BC, Nehemiah returns 445 BC

Context: We are in the last days of the Old Testament about 450 years before Christ. The people of Israel have been back in the Promised Land for almost a hundred years, but are still weak and fragile. God sends a trio of men to rebuild his people into a holy nation.

Walt had built video recorders in a factory for years. Now the company was shutting down, and he was out of a job. Walt got a job as a night watchman at half the salary but felt like he was going nowhere. He saw no future and wondered if he would ever feel good about himself again. It must have felt like that for the Jews who returned from Babylon. It took them about 20 years to rebuild the temple. Now, sixty years later, the nation is still dirt poor and are vassals to the Persian Empire far away. It seems like God has about forgotten them. God's answer is to send Ezra, Nehemiah, and Malachi to help rebuild his people. The nation will rise again so that it can be the home of the Messiah. In this last stop in the Old Testament, we see a loving Father care for His people.

God's first task was to rebuild the worship life of the nation. It had been 60 years since the temple had been rebuilt, but the Jews barely knew their God. God moved the Persian King to send Ezra the priest to begin this renewal. *"You are sent by the king and his seven advisers to inquire about Judah and Jerusalem with regard to the Law of your God"* Ezra 7:14 Ezra gathered priests and Levite descendants to help him bring the worship of God to the people. He was to teach the people God's word so that they might know their God again and not just go through the motions of worship. Ezra and the priests and Levites that he brought with him were to restore worship to Jerusalem. It is here in God's house that we all come to understand God and to honor him with our lives.

Worship was worthless without holiness, and so God began rebuilding the righteousness of his people. During the sixty years since the rebuilding of the temple, the people had slowly adopted the practices of their pagan neighbors. Ezra and Malachi warn them of the consequences. *"Judah has broken faith. A detestable thing has been committed in Israel and in Jerusalem: Judah has desecrated the sanctuary the Lord loves, by marrying the daughter of a foreign god." Mal.2:11* Having returned to worship in the temple, they now needed to return to worshipping the Lord with their lives. Disobedience had made the times tough during those sixty years. The prophets promised that God would provide for His people if they returned to Him.

A holy people needed a safe place to live. God put it on the heart of a man named Nehemiah to rebuild the walls of Jerusalem so that the people could worship God in peace. He went before the Persian emperor and asked for time and the resources to rebuild the walls. The enemies of the Jews did all that they could to keep the wall from being built. *"So the wall was completed on the twenty-fifth of Elul, in fifty-two days. When all our enemies heard about this, all the surrounding nations were afraid and lost their self-confidence, because they realized that this work had been done with the help of our God." Nehemiah 6:15-16.* The wall was rebuilt, and the nations were on notice that God's people were home.

Four or five days after the wall was built, there was one more thing to do. The faith of the nation had to be restored. God's people had to understand God's ways so that it could enter their hearts in this new-found city. For one whole morning, Ezra read the books of Moses to the people. *"He read it aloud from daybreak till noon as he faced the square before the Water Gate in the presence of the men, women and others who could understand." Nehemiah 8:3.* As the words of scripture were read, God reclaimed the hearts of his people. God wanted them to know His path for their lives. Actions are meaningless if they do not come from a heart that knows and loves God.

The pieces are in place, but now the real challenge of rebuilding is whether the people will rebuild their lives. Some argued with Malachi, Ezra, and Nehemiah about what it meant to return. Malachi offers a simple test. Are you giving of your time and resources to the Lord? God is still ready to commit to those who will commit to Him. He will bless those who open up their lives to him. As we close out the Old Testament, we can see the joy of people who have discovered what it is like to be loved again. No matter what your life is like, God wants to rebuild your faith and righteousness so that you can have that joy again. Take His challenge and open up your heart so that the Lord can bring joy back to your life as well.

- How would you rate the joy in your life? What would it take for you to open up your life so that the Lord could rebuild that happiness?

23
Unexpected Wisdom
Matthew 1-2, Luke 1-2
Jesus is born 6/5 BC

Context: It has been 400 years since the last of the Old Testament prophets have spoken. In the little town of Bethlehem will happen something so unexpected that the world still doesn't fully understand it.

Lord, why did you have to make that so hard? It should have been easy to have a children's night out program, yet everything that could have gone wrong did. We ran out of materials and had a group of kids that would not listen. Ministry is often not what we expect. It can be too hard or take too long. It can even bring surprises that are amazing. Such is the story of Christmas. While we routinely think of the manger, the shepherds and magi as part of the Christmas story, I doubt that it was what the Old Testament saints expected. There is a reason that many of the Jews of Jesus' day found it difficult to accept the birth narrative. God's plan contained pieces that they would never have conceived of. The story of the first Christmas, however, shows God's wisdom again and again.

We begin at the manger. No one in the Old Testament would have expected that the Messiah would be found in such poverty. *"And she gave birth to her firstborn, a son. She wrapped him in cloths and placed him in a manger because there was no room for them in the inn."* Luke 2:7. Jesus should be born in the palace for He is from the line of David. He should be trained to lead the nation back to the greatness of the days of David. God did the unexpected and made the Messiah available to all. Shepherds and townspeople surround Him at His birth. Every Jew will have access to the newborn king. He is the Lord of all.

Now turn to see his mother. She is an unmarried pregnant woman about to give birth to her first-born child. Mary probably carried the stigma of being a loose woman all her life. Mary was not the kind of woman that any good Jew would have expected for the mother of the Messiah. We know what the Old Testament Jews did not understand. *"The Holy Spirit will come upon you (Mary), and the power of the Most High will overshadow you. So the holy one to be born will be called the Son of God" Luke 1:35* This was not a harlot, but a virgin. God and not Joseph was the father of Jesus so that the child would be both man and God. He would be holy so that He could bear the sins of the world. God was again doing the unexpected.

Now turn to Jesus' Father. Joseph is given the role of protecting the Messiah. *"An angel of the Lord appeared to Joseph in a dream, "Get up," he said, "take the child and his mother and escape to Egypt" Matt 2:13* The child was vulnerable. Stories have grown up of the infant Jesus doing miracles as if He exhibited divine power from the start. The truth of the Bible is that God spoke to Joseph in dreams at least four times so that Joseph could take the child out of the harm of men like Herod and his son Archelaus. The child was hidden from His enemies first in Egypt and then in Galilee so that He could grow up in peace. There was a real danger that the salvation of the world might be lost if the child was to die prematurely. God used Joseph to protect the vulnerable child

Finally, turn to the magi. No Jew could have expected that these foreigners would be the first to see Jesus as God. *"On coming to the house, they saw the child with his mother Mary, and they bowed down and worshiped him." Matt 2:11* The shepherds praised God for what they had seen and heard on the night of His birth. The wise men went further. They bowed down and worshiped Jesus presenting Him with gifts that were fit for a deity. They alone in the Christmas story see Jesus as God. Here is the greatest surprise of all for the Old Testament Jew. Jesus would be the Savior of the whole world and not just be the king of the Jews. God did the unexpected and saved the world, not the nation.

One of the greatest lessons that we often miss is that God doesn't always do things as we expect. I think of the hardships that Mary and Joseph endured so that the birth of the Messiah was done God's way. God could have made it easier, but God's plan brought results that no Jew could ever have imagined. Sometimes ministry can take us in unexpected directions. God always has a reason. Jesus had to be born this way and not in any way that the Jewish church or even Disney could never imagine. He was to be God and man and be the savior of all. As we do our ministry, expect the unexpected. God wants to do miracles even if it is tougher than we want it to be. God has a plan beyond all our expectations. Submit to His will as Mary and Joseph did and God will do miracles through you.

- Where do you find your ministry to be difficult right now? What miraculous results might be possible if you followed God's plan instead of asking Him to follow yours?

24
Living in the Light
Matt 3-4, John 3-4
Jesus begins His ministry 26 AD

Context: Thirty years have passed since Jesus' birth. He has grown up in Nazareth quietly and without the world noticing. Now it is time for the ministry to begin and His teaching and miracles begin to start attracting crowds.

Light has a way of attracting us. We are instantly drawn to a campfire or a light on a starless night. Darkness can often bring fear or even cause us to stumble. Light, by comparison, brings comfort and draws us together with others. For four hundred years, the people had been living in darkness with no prophets of the Lord and few miracles. Then Jesus burst on the scene. His miracles were so numerous, and His teaching was so powerful that people could not ignore them. Crowds began to follow Him everywhere. Even the Jewish leaders who came to hate him could not dispute the miracles of healing, providing food or raising the dead. Here was one who spoke as if He knew God personally. Some would shy away from the light in Jesus day. Those who come into the light of Jesus will find new opportunities and joys.

After 400 years since the days of Malachi, God sent John to announce the light. He comes with power and proclaiming a message of repentance. *"In those days John the Baptist came, preaching in the Desert of Judea 2 and saying, "Repent, for the kingdom of heaven is near." Matt. 3:1-2.* Like an opening act at a rock concert, John warms up the dark and cold crowd for the light to come. He doesn't claim to be the light but prepares them for Jesus and His message. He also announces the Light's theme: change. Change is coming, and people need to be aware that things will not be just as they have always been. Men and women will have to make a choice. They can live in the light or reject it.

As Jesus begins His ministry, the light is powerful. Jesus does miracles never done before. Jesus healed the sick, raised the dead and fed thousands. He even commands Satan himself. Jesus said to him, *"Away from me, Satan! For it is written: 'Worship the Lord your God, and serve him only.'" Then the devil left him, and angels came and attended him." Matt. 4:10-11.* Notice that He doesn't deal with Satan with lightning bolts or divine power, but simply with three Bible passages. He is so powerful that the consequences of sin and the power of Satan in people's lives can be overcome by a mere word of His mouth. People flocked to the light of Jesus so that He might heal and help them in their darkness.

His focus was always the salvation of the people. Nicodemus, a leader of the Jewish people, came to have an intimate talk with Jesus away from the crowds. He and others had seen the power of Jesus' miracles. They had heard his teaching which was more powerful than any rabbi that they had heard. They wondered "Who was this man?" Jesus minced no words but got to the heart of the matter. *"For God did not send his Son into the world to condemn the world, but to save the world through him." John 3:17* His purpose was not to heal all human pain but to bring salvation from heaven. Out of the darkness, man will be brought into the light of the cross and its forgiveness and salvation.

This salvation was for all people. Jesus went to the Samaritans as well as the Jews. The woman at the well was a half breed with several divorces who was living in sin. By all the Jewish rules, she didn't belong in the kingdom of God. Even she is surprised with Jesus stops to talk with her and offer His love and forgiveness. She comes to believe and tells her whole community so that they accept Jesus as well. *"They said to the woman, "We no longer believe just because of what you said; now we have heard for ourselves, and we know that this man really is the Savior of the world." John 4:42.* All are to live in the light of Jesus.

Why live in darkness when you can live in the light. Sadly, there will be people who reject the light that Jesus brings. They will be happy to stumble in fear and darkness because they don't want the light that Jesus gives. Those who are attracted to the light will find that they have a guide in life. Jesus will give them courage and answers when they face the darkness of crisis. They will discover that His joy and peace will fill their lives as they turn up the wattage in life with daily prayer and Bible study. Light overcomes the darkness, and so the light of Jesus overcomes any darkness that Satan or the world want to bring into our lives. There is no reason for people to live in the darkness of Satan when the light of Jesus can change everything in their world. Live in the light and give the light to others so that they can have his power and salvation in their lives.

• Is the light of Jesus a bright bulb in your life or just a flickering candle? How will the light of Jesus guide your way? How might it show what is in the dark corners of your heart and mind?

25
No Ordinary Man
Gospels
Jesus' ministry 26-30 AD

Context: Over a three and a half year ministry, Jesus preached and healed people like no one had ever done before. The crowds followed Him, and many committed their lives to Him. Those who were touched by Him were never the same again.

Our culture is filled with self-proclaimed and media proclaimed heroes. They are athletes and movie stars and the ordinary guy who saves a woman from a burning car. They are our idols and we long to be extraordinary like them. Many of them don't seem unique for long. They grow old and weak or find themselves in a scandal that makes tarnishes their reputation. One person always was extraordinary and has remained so. His name is Jesus. He did things that no one else has ever done. He healed the blind and spoke like He knew God first hand. He had a way of making the ordinary people around Him extraordinary. Those who build their lives around Jesus will stand out as He mentors them. Those who spend their lives with Jesus will be extraordinary, too.

Jesus was wise beyond words. He did not teach like the Jewish teachers of the day. They taught out of a book sharing ideas of past scholars. Jesus taught God's word from His heart. *"The people were amazed at his teaching because he taught them as one who had authority, not as the teachers of the law."* Mark 1:22 Jesus is an extraordinary teacher who knows the truth about values and what is best in every situation. He is able to apply the message to the lives of His hearers in simple ways that they could understand and use. We would be wise to hang on every word that He says. His teaching gives people an edge in life. The words of Jesus are filled with insights about how to live with others, how to be a good employee and how to manage your money that works.

Jesus was able to help everyone with any problem that they faced. *"The people were amazed when they saw the mute speaking, the crippled made well, the lame walking and the blind seeing. And they praised the God of Israel." Matthew 15:31.* The days of miracles had seemed to have passed. Then Jesus burst on the scene, and the lame could walk, and the dead were raised. Even the wind and the wave was at His disposal. The number and scope of his miracles were like nothing that had ever been seen before. Jesus is still a great miracle worker and friend for those who come to Him in prayer. He is worth following so that we might have his support when life is good and His help when life is filled with troubles.

Jesus is stronger than the demons that we face. In Judah, Satan had the hearts and lives of many. He controlled them, and often they were naked, half crazed and out of control. The demons were afraid of Jesus. They cried out in fear when He came. When Jesus cast them out or commanded them to be quiet, they had to obey. *"All the people were amazed and said to each other, "What is this teaching? With authority and power, he gives orders to evil spirits, and they come out!" Luke 4:36* Life can easily be out of control for you and me. We may not believe in demons, but they are still around us. It can be the unreasonable person at work or a string of "coincidences" that are all bad luck. Jesus can handle it all.

Jesus has great compassion for the helpless. He was never too busy to help someone. *"When he saw the crowds, he had compassion on them, because they were harassed and helpless, like sheep without a shepherd." Matt. 9:36* Even when He was tired, He stopped to heal the mob of people begging for help. He saw their pain and how their illness had destroyed their bodies. It broke His heart. Jesus still has compassion for men and women like you and me. He hurts when you and I are feeling pain. Jesus grieves when someone dies too early or when a child doesn't have a meal all day. He is the friend that every person needs and who will always care about you.

Jesus is the friend that every one of us needs. When you get to know Him well, the extraordinary rubs off. The twelve disciples were changed by their time with Jesus and his abilities had become theirs. Even His enemies noticed the effect that He had on people. *"When they saw the courage of Peter and John and realized that they were unschooled, ordinary men, they were astonished, and they took note that these men had been with Jesus." Acts 4:13* Anyone who wants to be more amazing will want to spend time with Jesus. They will spend time studying the Bible and gain His wisdom for their life. They will time in service with Him so that they get to change lives miraculously. He is the mentor and friend that will take the time to help us to be our very best. There is no one like Jesus, and those who are close to Him will stand out in the crowd. They become wise and caring like Him.

• What qualities of Jesus amaze you the most? If you could have Jesus mentor you in one area of your life, what would it be?

26
Honored to Have a Friend
Gospels
Jesus' ministry 26-30 AD

Context: Jesus' ministry divided the Jewish people. The Pharisees and Sadducees hated Him and were jealous of His influence. The twelve disciples and others felt the love that He shared and were honored to be near Him.

If you know someone important, you usually make sure that everyone else knows. It may be that you had dinner with the president or that you went to high school with a major league baseball player. We all want our touch with the famous and powerful. While few can say that they are close to the president or a movie star, we do have the opportunity to be close to someone who is more powerful and famous than all of the people I have mentioned. We can be friends with Jesus. That relationship is often more special than we think. A lot of Christians treat their relationship with Jesus casually, but his desire to be close to us is very special and should be treasured.

It is easy to forget Jesus is God and was present at the time of creation. *"I tell you the truth," Jesus answered, "before Abraham was born, I am!"* John 8:58 Jesus rightfully speaks of God as Father, and here He claims to be older than Abraham. For two years, the people had seen His miracles of healing, demon casting, and feeding the masses. His works and teaching were undeniable, yet He seldom got the respect that was due. No one ever considered that He could be more than a prophet. We also often focus on His manhood more than His divinity. The first thing man has to learn about Jesus is our place before Him. Jesus is God and is not my equal.

Because He is God, He should be respected. I don't know why the demons give Jesus more respect than the humans, but they do. When he saw Jesus, he cried out and fell at his feet, shouting at the top of his voice, *"What do you want with me, Jesus, Son of the Most High God? I beg you, don't torture me!"* *Luke 8:28* Christians don't have to be afraid of Jesus like demons do because Jesus is not our enemy. We should listen to Him and respect Him because of His great power. He is the one who will battle the demons of life for us and heal us when we are sick. He has the wisdom of God and will give us answers that no one else can give. Honor Him for His willingness to come and help.

I should respect Jesus because He is not second to God, but is God. The Jewish leaders saw His miracles and wondered if He is the Messiah promised to come. The answer is, of course, yes, but He is more and he tells them plainly that He is one with God the Father. *"My Father, who has given them to me, is greater than all; no one can snatch them out of my Father's hand. I and the Father are one."* *John 10:29-30* Many have tried to treat Jesus as less than God. We need to acknowledge that He is almighty God who has humiliated himself to become man and save us. His humanness was not an act of desperation, but supreme power and love worthy of our worship.

The greatest reason to respect Him is that He is the giver of life. Our fate is in His hands. He is the judge we will face on the last day and the one who saved us by His cross. *"But these are written that you may believe that Jesus is the Christ, the Son of God and that by believing you may have life in his name."* *John 20:31* We are called to believe in Him because it will change our future. It is foolish to ignore Jesus or to demote Jesus to just another historical figure. Those who say all gods are alike miss the most crucial thing. Only Jesus has the power to save. The wise respect and believe in the words of scripture. He is the key to salvation, and we would be lost without Him.

He is not my equal. The wise will obey Him out of love and not out of fear. *"Jesus replied, "If anyone loves me, he will obey my teaching. My Father will love him,"* *John 14:23.* We have been loved by God Himself who has shown that He deeply cares about us and wants to bring us joy in life. I have always wondered why we humans think that we have the right to tell Jesus how to run the world or think that we can tell Him how our life should be. We are not even as powerful as the demons and maybe not as smart as they are. I would rather follow Jesus and have Him on my side guiding my life. Others may not think that they need Him, but I want to be in His throne room so that I can spend lots of time in prayer and listening to Him in His word. He is the son of God. As terrifying as His power should be, I will live content with Him for I know that He loves me, too.

- How do you show respect for Jesus? How willing are you to obey everything that He says or do you still find yourself questioning some of the things He commands?

27
He Came to Be a Savior
Matt 26-27, Mark 14-15, Luke 22-23, John 13-19
Good Friday 30 AD

Context: Jesus did so many amazing miracles. He taught as no one had taught before Him. Those were not the focus of His ministry. He came to be our Savior. His miracles and teachings were only a precursor to His work on a cross to save all mankind.

I walked into the church auditorium for an exciting conference on outreach and preaching. The speakers were first-rate, and the conference was sold out. I saw banners proclaiming some of the opportunities for members to work in the inner city with the homeless and posters for several missionaries that they were supporting. Something felt wrong as I sat down for the conference. I looked all around, and then it hit me. There was no cross in this building. It could have been a college lecture hall or symphony concert hall. Without the cross, you can't proclaim or understand Jesus. Jesus was a teacher and miracle worker, but it is the story of the cross that is central to His life and our faith. Sadly, not everyone wants a savior on a cross.

Some want a Savior who will give a comfortable life. On the way to the cross, Jesus takes three of the disciples up on a mountain for the transfiguration. On the mountain, they get a bit of heaven. Moses and Elijah are there, and Jesus is in all His glory. Trouble was far away, and the gates of heaven were opened. Peter wants to stay. *"Peter said to Jesus, "Lord, it is good for us to be here. If you wish, I will put up three shelters--one for you, one for Moses and one for Elijah." Matt. 17:4* Some still think that Jesus came to give the peaceful life. They are disappointed when life has problems or when ministry is tough. And when the Christian life is not easy, they think that

Jesus has failed. The real savior gives all of us something better than an easy life.

Some want a Savior who is the great provider. On Palm Sunday, we see Jesus is riding into Jerusalem on a colt. The people decided that the Messiah had come and was ready to take His throne in Jerusalem. *"Blessed is the king who comes in the name of the Lord!" "Peace in heaven and glory in the highest!" Luke 19:38* He would push out the Romans and would take over the throne of great King David. Peace and prosperity will be had by all men in Judea. Some still think of Jesus as the savior from our problems. Feeling sick, Jesus will cure you. Need a job; the answer is a simple prayer away. Many won't believe in Jesus if someone doesn't get well or that job doesn't come.

The real Jesus came to be a Savior from sin. He never said that His work as Savior was done with miracles or great teaching. His work was complete when He died on the cross. *"When he had received the drink, Jesus said, "It is finished." With that, he bowed his head and gave up his spirit." John 19:30* His death was what God had promised Adam and Eve in the garden and what God had continued to promise through the ages. The Savior had brought salvation. It is what all of us need. We enjoy the fellowship and it is great to have God's help when we need a job or feel sick. Yet, the greatest need we have is forgiveness. We need someone who will take away the guilt that haunts us from the past and the eternal death that haunts the future.

Many don't want to see the real savior. It isn't pretty to see His beaten and bloody body on the cross. It was something that few could bear to see on Good Friday. It was for this reason that Jesus came. Make Jesus just a great prophet who died too early in life or a caring man who helped many who were ill or hurting, and you miss the whole point of His life. That may be easier for us to handle because we don't want to admit our sin. The ultimate purpose of Jesus was to die for our sin. Everything else was secondary to Him and should be to us. The truth is that we are all sinners who sin daily and can't save ourselves. The heart of the Bible is that God sent His son to come and save us by His death and resurrection.

I look at the cross at the center of my church's altar and smile. The cross of Jesus changes everything. It is because of the cross that we have become people of God. All the other things that people want from Jesus are now possible from a Jesus, our savior. It would be my desire that everyone could have the joy that comes to us from the cross. Sin and guilt cause people a lot of pain. It is the forgiveness from the cross that overcomes our guilt and makes us free. Jesus helped a lot of men and women during His life, but the greatest thing He did was to die on the cross. If you don't know Jesus as the dying savior, you don't know the real Jesus.

- What do you want in a savior? What does it mean that Jesus died for you? How has the cross changed your life and your future?

28
Never Underestimate Jesus
Matt. 28, Mark 16, Luke 24, John 20-21
Easter 30 AD

Context: On the Sunday after Good Friday, the disciples were hopeless and hid in the upper room. The enemies of Jesus were gloating about finally getting rid of this rabbi who did miracles. No one expected a miracle that would change the world that day.

Expectations are everything. We often have high expectations for a Lexus or a Cadillac. However, I would not expect much excitement from a golf or tennis competition since I play neither game. What you expect colors your feelings. As you celebrate the resurrection of Jesus, how would you rate Easter compared to Christmas, Thanksgiving or even the Fourth of July? Sadly, a lot of people would prefer just to skip Easter. There are no football games, presents, or even fireworks on this holiday. Easter is a time of bunnies, colored eggs, and pastel dresses. Boring! Wait, don't write Easter off yet. I would submit that you have to understand Easter to see its value. What you expect of Easter often determines the blessings that you receive.

If you have low expectations of Easter, take heart. Both the friends and enemies of Jesus were not expecting much. His friends hid in the upper room trying to figure out how life without Jesus was going to look. Their hearts felt empty because the good times were over. His enemies thought they had beaten him, but feared a deception. *"So give the order for the tomb to be made secure until the third day. Otherwise, his disciples may come and steal the body and tell the people that he has been raised from the dead."* Matt. 27:64 Jesus' enemies never thought He would rise from the dead as He had said, but they wanted to prevent a hoax from happening. Resurrection was the last thing on their minds.

On Easter, everyone saw how great He is. The women came expecting to finish embalming a dead body. Jesus had told them that He would rise again, but no one believed it. With sad and heavy hearts they came to finish the burial. To their surprise, they saw angels who had a message. *"He is not here; he has risen, just as he said. Come and see the place where he lay." Matt. 28:6* Jesus was not their dead friend, but a living Savior. He had risen just as He said He would. He is the Almighty Son of God who had come to save the world from sin. God had higher expectations of Easter than anyone else. Jesus is bigger than we think.

Two disciples heard the news that Jesus had risen but just couldn't believe it. It didn't make sense. Leaving Jerusalem, their minds were confused when they met a stranger. They told him how they had hoped that Jesus would change their life, but their hopes were shattered. The stranger replied, *"Did not the Christ have to suffer these things and then enter his glory?" Luke 24:26.* The stranger with them was Jesus Himself, and He began to explain to them how the Messiah had to suffer if the promises of salvation were going to be true. It was a moment that changed their expectations of the cross. They rushed back to Jerusalem to share the news with the others. Jesus was alive.

The resurrection was just the beginning. Jesus had higher expectations for the future. *"You are witnesses of these things. I am going to send you what my Father has promised." Luke 24:48-49* The disciples had seen something special, and they were to share their witness about what Jesus had done. Jesus wanted to change the world and give them the gift of salvation. The resurrection was just the beginning. Easter would transform the world. It would bring mercy to those weighed down with sin. It would bring eternal life and spare those who believe from the pain of hell. It was truly a day to celebrate and tell the world about what Jesus had done.

The disciples came to this day with heartache. They didn't

expect anything special to happen. You and I don't have to make that same mistake. We come to Easter each year knowing that we will celebrate His gift of life for us. Easter has changed everything. Just ponder for a moment what life would be like without Easter. There would be no forgiveness, and you and I would be bound for hell. Realize that millions of people across the earth are in that predicament. Easter doesn't exist for them because no one has shared the story of Easter with them. They still don't expect much from Easter.

You can change their future just like the disciples did. On Easter Day, there was only a handful who knew what Jesus had done. That was soon to change. It is estimated that a million people believed in the resurrection by the year 100 AD and that by 350 AD, Christianity had conquered the Roman Empire. The message did change lives, and it can transform the lives of the people around you if you tell them. Let their expectations be high. Look beyond the bunnies and the Easter Eggs to what Jesus has done. Easter is all about expectations. If you expect much, it will be the greatest day of the year.

• Who do you know who is not impressed with Easter? What impresses you enough about the resurrection that you will take the time to share it with them?

29
Now What?
Acts 1-8
Pentecost 30 AD

Context: Starting with Pentecost which was only 50 days after Easter, the early church had an exciting mission to do. They were to take the message of Easter out into the world so that the gospel could change the world.

Easter is over – Now What? Something great had happened at Easter. It was time for the next movement in God's plan. The book of Acts records how the disciples followed Jesus for forty days after Easter. It was like old times. He taught them, and he did miracles before them. Now it was different. He walked through walls; he didn't need to sleep. Before Easter, they thought that they knew the nature of ministry. Now they were not sure. *"So when they met together, they asked him, "Lord, are you at this time going to restore the kingdom to Israel?"* Acts 1:6 They didn't realize the wave that was coming. The church often forgets that Easter left us a job to do. The early chapters of the book of Acts are a call to arms and a pattern for the church to get on fire.

The "what is next" for the church is to witness. The problem was that the early church was not yet ready for this task. Jesus would prepare them for this task. He promised that they would receive power to be witnesses. *"But you will receive power when the Holy Spirit comes on you; and you will be my witnesses in Jerusalem, and in all Judea and Samaria, and to the ends of the earth."* Acts 1:8 The Holy Spirit would come on them mightily on Pentecost. In preparation for that day, the people would pray continually for ten days. They would open themselves up to the Spirit's power for they knew that something big was happening. Prayer is still the way that the church prepares to bring Easter to the world.

Pentecost was the dawning of a new day. The tongues of fire lit upon the disciple's heads, and the disciples were on fire as well proclaiming the message of Easter. *"God has raised this Jesus to life, and we are all witnesses of the fact."* Acts 2:32 Having received power from God, the disciples told what they had seen and heard. The Holy Spirit worked upon the hearts of those who were present for the festival of Pentecost. 3000 people came to faith that day because Peter spoke what God had revealed to him. The church is still to let the message explode through our world. It is up to us to find others who do not know that message. People need to hear what Jesus has done for them.

Witnessing takes effort, and we will soon grow tired. Like rechargeable batteries, God's people need to recharge their power if they were going to witness in tough times. *"They devoted themselves to the apostles' teaching and to the fellowship, to the breaking of bread and to prayer"* Acts 2:42 They devoted themselves to Bible study and prayer letting the power of the Lord fill their lives. Prayer was not a one-time event, it was ongoing in the church. As they were in the word, "the Lord added to their number daily." Here is a model for the church. It is to be a people connected daily with the Lord so that His power energizes the witness.

A powerful movement will meet resistance. Thousands had soon become Christians, and the worried Jewish leaders arrested Peter and John and told them to stop preaching about Jesus. The power of Jesus couldn't be stopped. *"But Peter and John replied, "Judge for yourselves whether it is right in God's sight to obey you rather than God. For we cannot help speaking about what we have seen and heard."* Acts 4:19-20 When the power comes on God's people, they don't just do witnessing; they become witnesses. Their whole life is about the wonder of the cross. They live it by showing kindness to others like the disciples did. They have a new joy in their lives that just has to be expressed.

Easter is over – Now What? Often Christians think that

when Easter is over, it is time to go back to our ordinary lives. Easter is just the beginning. It is the message that must burst forth from every Christian. Be in the word and prayer so that you can recharge your spiritual batteries. You will find it hard to share the message if you have no Godly power in you. Commit yourself to daily time in prayer and Bible study. Be praying and Bible people like the church after Pentecost.

And as you are being fed, let your light shine. Live in such a way that people see your good works and give glory to God in heaven. Live in such a way that people know you are a Christian and ask you to pray for them. Easter is over - Now what? The answer is simple. Live in the light of Easter as you power up through Bible study and prayer so that your life doesn't have to be ruled by the darkness. Then let your light shine so that Easter can dispel the darkness that has taken over the world. Easter is powerful and can change the world one person at a time.

- Who do you know who does not understand the Easter story? What are two things that you would tell them about Easter that could change their lives?

30
The Church Expands
Acts 9-16
Paul's first missionary journey 46-48 AD

Context: The first seven chapters of the book of Acts focus on the ministry in Jerusalem, but persecution and the story of Saul (who we know as Paul) show that the Lord was forcing His church to mature so that she could carry out His purpose of the world's salvation.

There is a progression to life. A baby becomes a toddler, a student in grade school, and all too soon a parent is sending their child off to college or trade school. It is hard in one respect, but it the natural progression. You wouldn't want that 40-year-old living in your basement, would you mom and dad? I was glad to see my children go to college, get their first job, get married and buy their first home. It was hard at times, but it has also been fulfilling. They have become adults in every sense of the word. God had a plan for His church to grow and mature. It would have been wrong for the church to stay limited to a few hundred or even thousand in Jerusalem. While the church grew in many directions, we see this growth in the story of Paul told in Acts. His ministry demonstrates the Lord's process of taking the baby church and letting it mature into a force that would change the world.

The story in Acts begins with a single heart only three years after the first Easter. God changed one man's heart as God started a movement. Saul was a persecutor of the church and was one of those who did not want any changes to the Old Testament way of doing things. God stepped in with a blinding light and a disabling blindness. God had a plan for this Saul. He told Ananias, "*Go! This man is my chosen instrument to carry my name before the Gentiles and their kings and before the people of Israel*". *Acts 9:15*. The man who was persecuting the church would become the great messenger of the Gospel. God changes hearts so the church can reach the world.

For sixteen years, the gospel had been centered in Palestine. Now it was time for the church to move beyond Judea and Syria. God had a plan. *"Set apart for me Barnabas and Saul for the work to which I have called them."* Acts 13:2 God called Paul and Barnabas to take the message out into the world. The church at Antioch would be their base and give them support for the ministry. It was time to head up into Asia Minor and reach names that roll off our tongues like the Galatian, Colossian and Ephesian peoples. God still wants His people to move out of their comfort zone into the places where the gospel message is needed. The gospel was never meant to be contained.

The success of the ministry can make us uncomfortable. The early church wrestled with the ministry to the Gentiles. Many wanted the Gentiles to follow all of the Jewish laws and customs. After solemn prayer, they made a decision. *"It is my judgment, therefore, that we should not make it difficult for the Gentiles who are turning to God. Acts 15:9.* Paul and others in the church felt led by God to give the gospel to the Gentiles without them having to become Jewish. God was showing that He wanted all the world to have salvation. God still pushes His church to reach out to people who are different than we are. The gospel message is a gift to all men and women.

God was not satisfied. It was time to move beyond Asia. As Paul returned to Asia Minor (Turkey) to encourage the churches there, God sent him a vision. *"During the night Paul had a vision of a man of Macedonia standing and begging him, "Come over to Macedonia and help us." Acts 16:9.* God wanted the message to travel to Greece and on to the rest of Europe. God moved him moved him westward into Europe with the Philippians, the Thessalonians, and the Corinthians. God is still calling us to proclaim the message onto new continents and around the world. The news of the empty tomb in Jerusalem was now a global phenomenon.

The church has to grow and continue to mature. It was never meant to be trapped in a culture or a place. When a child doesn't grow into a mature adult, we know that there is something wrong. When the church is stuck in one locale or refuses to interact with its world, there is something wrong as well. When the early church found it hard to move out of the comfort of Jerusalem, God allowed persecution to disperse His people. The pain soon became a blessing. God will not permit the church to stay trapped in its ways. He wants the world to know what Jesus did on the cross for all of us. He will encourage us to get out of our comfort zone to share with the world. We don't have to be St. Paul to share, but God wants His church to grow and mature so that they can bring the power of the gospel to the world that is in need.

• How have you and your church reached outside your walls and shared the gospel with the world around you? What holds you back and what blessings could God bring if you were willing to reach out?

31
Mission Becomes Legacy
Acts 16-28
Paul's execution 68 AD

Context: Paul would be martyred in Rome in 68AD, but his voice continues to speak. His legacy is not in the statues or stain glass windows but in the people and writings that continue to this day. His impact on the church and every Christian can't be denied.

Every person should have a legacy. Some people have their legacies put into stone or bronze like the four presidents on Mount Rushmore. Washington, Jefferson, Lincoln, and Teddy Roosevelt all made lasting contributions to our nation and are remembered by a grateful nation on the side of a mountain. Other people have their legacy shared by someone who loved them and who were touched by them at their funeral. Sadly, far too many die without any lasting legacy. They are gone, and people struggle to tell how they changed the world for the better. St. Paul was one of those who had a legacy that touches every living Christian today. Few of us have not been affected by the books of Roman, Corinthians or Philippians. Many of us look to his example in life as a guide for our ministry. Christians like you and I can have a lasting legacy with our families and the people we have touched. Today we will look at Paul's legacy and ours.

Paul had a lasting legacy in the many people that he touched. *"Timothy, my fellow worker, sends his greetings to you, as do Lucius, Jason and Sosipater, my relatives." Romans 16:21* The end of the book of Romans mentions twenty-six people who had ministered with Paul. Some are names we know well. Others are only referred to in the Bible here. All had a significant impact on the church. His heart and life touched them, and they were witnesses together of the gospel. Everyone was better because of their time with Paul. Christians are not to work in isolation. Our ministry is not just to complete the task, but to minister to each other. We leave a piece of ourselves with each other.

It wasn't long before the churches that Paul planted got to be so many that he could not minister to them all. Paul sent Titus to Crete, Timothy to Ephesus, Crescens went to Galatia, and many others into the world. Paul multiplied the ministry by training and sending coworkers across the mission field. *"The reason I left you in Crete was that you might straighten out what was left unfinished and appoint elders in every town, as I directed you." Titus 1:5* Each of these people were mentored by Paul and would, in turn, mentor others for ministry. Paul set a pattern that we should replicate today. There were no seminaries. People worked with Paul and would continue the ministry even when he was gone.

They could chain Paul up, but they could not silence His faith. *"I, Paul, write this greeting in my own hand. Remember my chains. Grace be with you." Col. 4:18* Thirteen Letters of Paul are included in the Bible, and Paul mentions others in the letters we have. His letters multiplied his ministry as one church got the letter and then copies of the letter went out to other churches around them. Even after Paul was martyred, his letters continued to speak his witness on behalf of the Lord. Today, his letters still touch our hearts and strengthen our faith. They have become his personal legacy to us. We sense Paul's faith and his intimate knowledge of God's wisdom and plan, and it changes our lives.

One of the greatest legacies that Paul ever left was the example of his life. Second Timothy is the last letter that Paul ever wrote, and it talks about his upcoming death. *"For I am already being poured out like a drink offering, and the time has come for my departure."* *2 Tim. 4:6* The message is simple: Timothy, follow the example of my life in which have participated and witnessed. It was in life that Paul had shown Timothy what it meant to be a child of God. The example of Paul's life still teaches us about Christian character and love. All the degrees and accolades don't mean as much as the example that you showed others and the way that you poured yourself out in life.

There is no reason that every Christian can't have a legacy. It begins with your family. You teach your children and are an example to your nieces and nephews of the character of God's people. They teach it to the next generation, and they teach it to the following generation and so on. You share your faith with a friend, and you may impact a whole family. You may not write books or start churches as Paul did but you can influence people with your witness and your life. Legacy is all about people. It may be the friend you sat with at the hospital or the children's program at your church that touched several families and brought them closer to the Lord. The faith and life that you live can make a difference with people for generations to come. They will welcome you in heaven and share a legacy that you might not even have realized that you had. Legacy begins now. What we do today can have an impact for generations to come.

• Who has had the deepest impact on your life? Who could you pass your faith on to and begin the legacy of God's love?

32
Hold On!
Book of Revelation
John wrote Revelation in 95 AD

Context: Sixty years have passed since the cross and the church is being persecuted. John, the beloved disciple of Jesus, sees a vision of God's glory and victory. God tells John to send this letter to seven churches in Asia so that they and we can be encouraged to hold on.

The score was 21 to 3 at halftime and the Bengals were losing. Everyone else in the room was angry and ready to give up on the Bengals. Yet, you felt calm and confident. You were certain that the Bengals will pull it out. Why? This is a rebroadcast of the game that you saw the day before. Your team scores 28 points in the second half while shutting down the opposition. The final score is certain. The book of Revelation is an appeal to people to have the same confidence that you do about the game. In the midst of persecution and Satan's attacks, it doesn't look good for the church. Yet, Revelation shows how things will end. In an age where many are leaving the church because ministry can be tough, we face the same question as the persecuted early church. "Do you want to be on the losing side?" If not, hold on and let the vision of John show you how things are going to end.

The early Christians had given up on God. *"Yet I hold this against you: You have forsaken your first love."* Rev. 2:4 Sixty years had passed since Christ's crucifixion. Most of the first generation Christians were gone. The second generation did not have their conviction and confidence. The seven letters to the churches show how Satan was chipping away at the church. The once strong church of Asia Minor was slipping away. This book begins with a plea for the church to hold on. Do not give into persecution or apathy. The message speaks loudly in an age when many have lost their love for Jesus. Satan is pulling the American church from the Lord with busyness and doubts.

The book of Revelation has several reasons for you to hang on to your faith. First, God has already won the first battle. Through the cross of Jesus, God has saved both the Jew and the Gentile from the coming wrath here on earth and on the last day. John looks at the saints in heaven and is told *"These are they who have come out of the great tribulation; they have washed their robes and made them white in the blood of the Lamb. Rev. 7:14* John is pleading with the people to not throw away the Easter victory that is theirs in Christ. You may face challenges, but those who cling to the cross will be victorious.

The future does not look good and we need someone to help us through the trials. Revelation is filled with waves of famine, war, and seas of blood. We see the destruction on the evening news each night. It is the result of a world filled with sin in which men kill each other and people starve in the aftermath. It is the world that will face the wrath of God for their sin. *"Then I heard a loud voice from the temple saying to the seven angels, "Go, pour out the seven bowls of God's wrath on the earth.""* *Rev. 16:1* God will allow these things to happen to break down man's pride so that some may come to faith and be saved. The Lord is our only hope. Hold on to Him in these trying times.

The final result is not in doubt. Satan and his armies will be destroyed. *"And the devil, who deceived them, was thrown into the lake of burning sulfur, where the beast and the false prophet had been thrown."* *Rev. 20:10* False hopes based on the work of men and false gods will be gone. Technology and governments that people think will provide the answers will be destroyed. Satan himself and his angels will be judged and spend eternity in hell. Many think that Satan is winning and will throw their lot in with him. He can't win the war because he cannot overcome the Lord. When the dust settles at the end, it will only be God and His people that are left standing.

For those who do hold on, there is a vision of what the future will look like. *"Then I saw a new heaven and a new earth, for the first heaven and the first earth had passed away, and there was no longer any sea."* *Rev. 21:1* Heaven is a beautiful place filled with God's people living and communing with God. It can be your new home. By holding up the future for the people of Asia Minor and for those living today, God is encouraging us to hold on. The suffering will be worth it because the prize is so great. God wants us to see that He is greater than all the scary things that are coming in the future. He wants you to hold on and let him help you through the coming trials. Revelation is a plea not to give up on God. God is your future and you can be certain how things will end for those who never let

Him go.

- What frustrations do you face because of your Christian faith?
  What difference does it make knowing that God is in control of the
  future?

Student Bible studies
The author gives permission for the student Bible studies to
be copied for local church or small group use

02
Abraham tested
Gen. 22:1-19

Abraham had many choices to make. His story begins with a decision to set out with his family for a strange land because of a promise from the Lord. All he had, in the beginning, was the incredible promises of God (Gen. 12). In the gift of Isaac, those promises had a face and future. Now, 40 years later, God calls Abraham to make a choice even more demanding than the first. It was a decision that required that he believed that God could keep those promises even if Isaac died.

God sent Abraham to the land of Moriah which is probably modern day Jerusalem, about 50 miles from where he was living. He would arrive on the third day which gave Abraham a lot of time to turn back or change his mind. This chapter records the greatest test that Abraham ever faced. I am sure that Abraham and Isaac came down the hill different men. Abraham becomes the man of God who trusts the Lord and becomes the model for the Jews in years to come. Isaac becomes the faithful patriarch who trusts the Lord with only one failure mentioned in the bible (Gen. 26). This test that seems so shocking taught them both the mercy and love of God.

1. What possession would be hardest for you to give up?

2. What command does God give to Abraham in verse 2? What is at stake for Abraham if Isaac dies?

3. How does Abraham respond to this command? (v.3)

4. What do you picture Abraham thinking as he hears and responds to this command? Why do you think that Abraham did not object to God's command?

5. How would you feel if you were asked you to make a big sacrifice for your ministry?

6. How far away is Moriah (v.4)? How would this make the test more difficult?

7. Many think that Isaac is a teenager at the time of the test. What question does he ask (v.7) and how does Abraham answer (v.8)?

8. On the mountain, how does Abraham show the depth of his faith? (v.10) Do you think that Abraham would have killed his son?

 9. When does God stop the sacrifice (v.11) and what can we learn from God's timing?

10. How does God provide the sacrifice as Abraham said he would (v.13)?

11. What does Abraham's example teach us about trusting the Lord enough to obey Him in every situation?

03
Joseph Reveals Himself
Gen. 45:1-28

The story of Joseph is the story of God taking a selfish man and developing a patriarch who would save his people. Along the way, he was betrayed and deserted by his family, exposed to sexual temptation, punished for doing the right thing, imprisoned, and forgotten by those he helped. As Joseph took each step, he grew into the leader that God was calling him to be. His attitudes were transformed, and people began to see the hand of God in him. Finally, he was ready to be the leader that God envisioned.

In Genesis 25, we see how completely Joseph had changed as he greets his brothers after many years. While they expected punishment for their crimes against him, he embraces them and weeps at the reunion with his family. He understands that God had sent him ahead to preserve the family. Joseph tells his brothers, "You intended to harm me, but God intended it all for good. He brought me to this position so I could save the lives of many people" (Genesis 50:20). The brother who had boasted to others about dreams had exchanged his dreams for the dreams God had for his family and the future.

1. What are family reunions or holidays like with your family? Is there someone that has been missing that you would like to see?

2. Judah has just offered his life for the life of Benjamin to save his father Jacob tremendous pain (Gen. 44:18-34). How does this show of mercy affect Joseph? (45:1-2)

3. When Joseph reveals himself to his brothers, what is their response? (45:3) What would it take for you to believe that someone was a lost relative who you thought was long dead?

4. How did God transform the evil that they had done into a blessing for the family (45:4-7)

5. How does God sometimes help us by allowing us to go through adverse circumstances?

6. What are Josephs' plans for his family? (45:9-13) Who does Joseph want to see?

7. Has Joseph truly forgiven his brothers? What leads you to think so?

8. As Joseph reveals himself, what does his message expose about the character of God?

9. What could you tell people about God from the story of your life? Why would that be a powerful witness?

10. Compare the young Joseph who mocked his brothers (Gen 37) to the Joseph in chapter 45. What has Joseph learned at the hand of God?

11. What adversities are you facing in your life? What lessons do you think God may be trying to teach you?

07
The Lord Prepares Joshua
Josh 1:1-18

Joshua was one of only two men who left Egypt in the Exodus and entered the Promised Land 40 years later. He became the assistant of Moses who stood at the foot of Mount Sinai waiting for the Ten Commandments. When Moses sent spies to scout out the land of Canaan, Joshua was selected as the representative of the tribe of Ephraim. He and Caleb alone believed that the Lord could conquer this place for His people. At Moses' death, Joshua was chosen by God to be Moses' successor and to lead the people to conquer the land that God promised to His people.

We find the Israelites camped east of the Jordan River across from the Promised Land. Having mourned for Moses, it is now time to move forward. God approaches Joshua and calls him to lead over a million people into the land that He promised them. While Joshua had been the assistant of Moses, the challenge must have been overwhelming. God pledges to be with Joshua as He was with Moses. The Lord challenges Joshua to study and obey the scripture which Moses has left behind. To be successful, you need to follow the Lord and listen to what He says.

1. When have you experienced a significant change in your life?

2. What is the context of our story and what does that mean for Joshua? (1:1-2)

3. When have you felt overwhelmed by a task that someone gave you? How did you cope?

4. What promise did the Lord give to Joshua (1:3-6) what conditions did God put on the promises?

5. What promises has God given you for your ministry?

6. Why was it important for Joshua to be "strong and courageous"? (1:6)

7. What commands does God give Joshua in verses 6-9?

8. How courageous do you feel in ministry right now? How does your courage in ministry or lack of courage affect your fellow servants?

9. Why is meditating on God's word so important for Joshua if he is to be courageous? Why does it matter to you?

10. How does Joshua show that he believes the promises that God has made? (1:10)

11. How do the people respond to Joshua? (1:16)

12. What challenge lies before you right now? What do you need to do so God can prepare you for success?

09
Ruth Meets Boaz
Ruth 2:1-23

A woman from the pagan nation of Moab, Ruth became the mother of Obed and great-grandmother of King David. Her story set during the time of the Judges reminds us that God wants to change our hearts so that He can change our circumstances. God is not here to make us comfortable. He desires to change us from the inside so that we can have the attitudes and values of His people. Ruth who begins outside the nation of Israel shows true loyalty to the Lord that is missing throughout much of the time of the Judges. It is her character and her faith that allows the Lord to remake her life and choose her to be one of the ancestors of Jesus.

The Book of Ruth tells the story of a Jewish family that leaves Israel during a time of a famine and has life go from bad to worse. All three men in the family die leaving Naomi and Ruth in a desperate situation. Returning to Judah, it is Ruth who leads the family back into God's promises by her willingness to work and to trust the Lord. She will marry Boaz and become part of God's chosen people. No one is outside God's grace and mercy if they will but trust in Him.

1. Have you ever lived or worked on a farm? What was your fondest memory?

2. How does Ruth provide for herself and Naomi (2:2) What dangers might she face by working there?

3. If you suddenly had no means of supporting yourself, how would you react? What can we learn from Ruth about being calm and taking advantage of opportunities?

4. Who is Boaz and what kind of man do you think he was? (2:4-5)

5. How Did Boaz's foreman describe Ruth (2:6-7)

6. What character traits of Ruth stand out to you? How would those qualities give an advantage to any Christian?

7. What specific instructions did Boaz give to Ruth, and how did she respond to him? (2:8-11) How do they each show respect for the other?

8. What reason did Boaz give Ruth for his particular attention to her? (2:11-12)

9. How did God show His faithfulness to Ruth and Naomi?

10. How did Naomi respond to Ruth's success (2:19-20) How does Ruth's success changer Naomi's view of the future from when she first arrived in Judea? (1:20)

11. Judging from the events in this story, what character traits does God honor in His people? How does your life reflect these character traits?

12. How have you opened yourself to God's miracles in your life?

11
David Spares Saul
1 Sam 24:1-22

David was the youngest of eight brothers in the city of Bethlehem. He was the keeper of his father's sheep and is well known for the many psalms that are attributed to him. David would rise to fame for killing the giant Goliath and soon was a general for Saul, the first king of the united Israel. He soon fell out of favor as Saul became jealous of David and his success. He would spend years as a fugitive before Saul's death in battle elevated David to succeed him as king.

The story in this text happens during the days when David was a fugitive being pursued by Saul. He and his men were hiding in a large cave in Southern Israel to escape Saul's pursuit. Saul enters the cave alone to relieve himself, and David faces the temptation to end the pursuit by killing Saul. His actions that day showed the character of David to Saul and David's men. It showed why the Lord had chosen David to succeed Saul and lead the people of God as King.

1. How does it feel when you suddenly have a rival or enemy at your mercy? What are you tempted to do?

2. What is the setting for our story and why has Saul come to this remote area? (24:1-2)

3. Why did Saul enter the cave where David and his men were hidden? (9:3) What did David's men think God was doing? (9:4)

4. Why does David cut off part of Saul's robe? Why is his conscience bothered when he only cut a piece of cloth? (24:4-5)

5. When have you found restraint speaking louder than actions? What are often the consequences of taking matters into your own hands?

6. When Saul left the cave, what does David do and why did he leave the cave? (24:8)

7. Why is it not enough to just confess our sin to the Lord? Why do we need to admit what we have done to the person that we hurt?

8. What proof did David give concerning his character? (24:11) What does David call on the Lord to do for him? (24:12,15)

9. How does Saul respond to David's words? (24:16-21) What does he know and what request does he make of David?

10. As you think about how the story plays out in the next couple of chapters, what is the difference between Saul and David? How have you seen the Godly triumph and the wicked defeated?

11 As you look at this story, how does God used trials and tests to shape His people?

13
Solomon Asks for Wisdom
1 Kings 3:1-15

His annual income was 25 tons of gold a year, and riches were all around him. He sat on an ivory throne overlaid with gold, received tribute from kings and merchants and drank from goblets made of gold. He was so rich that silver had almost no value in the days of Solomon. The queen of Sheba came like many others to see if the rumors were true and found that his wisdom and riches exceeded every tale. She declared that those who lived in the kingdom of Solomon were incredibly blessed to live in such a kingdom of riches, peace, and wisdom.

When Solomon ascended the throne, the people of Israel soon learned that he was not another David. He was a scholar, not a soldier, a man more interested in erecting buildings than fighting battles. This passage is the story of the opportunity that God gave to Solomon to be as great a ruler as his father, David. He chooses wisely in this story, but there are already hints of the women that would weaken his resolve for the Lord. Solomon would live in luxury with treaties with many nations even as Solomon would realize that wisdom and wealth were not enough to bring happiness. (Eccl. 12:13-14)

1. If a genie gave you a single wish, what choice would you make?

2. David had conquered the nations on the battlefield. Solomon chose diplomacy by marrying the daughters of foreign kings. What country is first to give their princess to Solomon (3:1) and what is the outcome of the marriage? (3:3)

3. Where does Solomon go early in his ministry and how does he show where his heart is at this point in his life? (3:4)

4. What did God say to Solomon? (3:5) How is this not only an incredible opportunity for Solomon but also a test of Solomon's heart and character?

6. What is Solomon's petition and how does he preface his request? (3:6-9)

7. Because God was pleased with Solomon's request, what other gifts did God give Solomon? (3:10-13)

8. What conditional promise does God make with Solomon? (3:14) Why was obedience so essential for the continuation of the blessings that the Lord was giving Solomon?

9. After Solomon had built and dedicated the temple, God would come to him with another promise in 1 Kings 9:4-7. What are God's promise and God's warning for Solomon?

10. Unfortunately, the wisest man that the world has ever had did not keep the promise to obey the Lord all his life. Why is obedience such a key to enjoying all the blessings that the Lord has given? (Eccl. 2:10-11)

11. What interests are close to your heart? Is there a decision that you are facing now that needs the wisdom that only God can give?

18
Daniel in the Lion's Den
Daniel 6:1-28

His ministry would span from the time he was taken by
Nebuchadnezzar as a teenager in 605 BC until the first year of
Cyrus in 536 BC. He and his three friends were examples of
faith to generations that struggled with a lack of faith. Their
devotion to the Lord brought them to the highest levels of
foreign governments and gave them opportunities to witness
to kings and nations how exceptional the real God was. Daniel
was a man of honesty and prayer. Foreigners recognized
Daniel's character and praised the true God because of what
they saw in Daniel and learned from him.

At the time of this text, Daniel was over 80 years old and
had become one of top three administrators in the nation. He
attracted the attention of King Darius because of his honesty
and ethics leading Darius to desire to put Daniel above all the
other leaders. A trap is set for Daniel, but Daniel will not give
up the worship of His God to save himself. His trust in the
Lord gives God the opportunity to show the world that He is
the true God. It also shows His great love for His prophet near
the end of Daniel's life.

1. Under what conditions would you consider stepping into a
lion's cage?

2. Why did Daniel's colleague's plot against him? (6:3-4) How
did they plan to discredit Daniel? (6:5)

3. How did Daniel respond to the king's decree? (6:9-10) What
motivated Daniel to respond that way?

4. What would Daniel have lost if he had given up praying to
the Lord for the 30 days of the edict?

5. Where is your faith challenged in life? What is at stake if you overcome the challenge or give in to trials to your faith?

6. Why is the king so distressed (6:14) What is the king's hope for Daniel? (6:16)

7. What happened during the night? (6:18-22)

8. Why doesn't God save every Christian who is persecuted?

9. Why do you think God saved Daniel? (6:23) How did God's deliverance of Daniel affect the king?

10. What happened to Daniel's accusers and their families? (6:24) Why do you think the King punished them?

11. When have you experienced trials for your faith? How has God helped you through those times of trial and trouble?

20
Mordecai Persuades Esther
Esther 4:1-17

The story of Esther begins in 483 about 100 years after the Fall of Jerusalem and 50 years after the first group of Jews has returned to Jerusalem. The Persians are in power and Judea is just a vassal state miles away from the palace where our story will occur. It is important to realize how powerless the Jews are at this point. Whatever the Persian king says is law, and it must be obeyed. While God is never mentioned directly in the book, there is no doubt that God is working to save His people. Esther becomes queen in an unlikely series of events, and God uses her words and actions to overturn an evil plot against his people.

What is this plot? The new prime minister has a long-time grudge against the Jewish people and has paid the king for the right of exterminating the Jews. Jews all over the kingdom are wailing and wearing sackcloth. Since the Persian Empire stretches from India to Ethiopia, there are few places for the people to run. Jews all over the kingdom are concerned about the race being wiped off the earth. Esther is the story of how God can change the world if one person is willing to take a risk.

1. When have you taken a risk and had it work out better than you thought it would?

2. In Esther 3:13, an edict from the king was made. What was the edict that is the background for all of chapter 4?

3. How do Mordecai and the other Jews react to the news? (4:1-4)

4. How have you reacted to an injustice to you or to Christians who are persecuted because of their faith?

5. Mordecai refused to be appeased by new clothes from Esther. His refusal of clothes caught her attention. What was Mordecai's message and what did Mordecai ask Esther to do? (4:6-9)

6. How does Esther reply to Mordecai? (4:11) Do you think she was denying Mordecai's request or is it something else?

7. How does Mordecai respond to Esther's message? (4:12-14)

8. What is the problem with just ignoring evil?

9. How does Mordecai show that he believes that God will deal with the problem no matter what Esther does? (4:14) What does this say about God's control of the future?

10. What is Esther's request so that she can prepare to see the king? (4:15-16)

11. In what kind of situations would it be good for Christians to fast and pray?

23
Jesus Walks on Water
Matthew 14:22-34

The Gospel writers recorded only a fraction of the miracles that Jesus did. He raised the dead, healed the sick, cast out the demon, and showed his power over nature. There was nothing that He could not do. Often, His heart was touched by the pain of those who were suffering. He would stop what he was doing just to help those in need. His miracles were proof that He was from God and drew people to come and listen to the message that He shared.

The Gospel of John tells us why Jesus sent His disciples away after the feeding of the five thousand. Jesus knew that the people wanted to make Him king and He did not want the disciples to fall under the desires of the crowd. On the water, they faced a storm and learned of the Lord's concern for them and the depth of His power. Peter reaches out to the Lord so that he can experience God's power and not just see it. He begins to sink when he takes his eyes off Jesus. This miracle can teach us to lean on Jesus through the storms of our lives.

1. What is the scariest experience that you have ever faced?

2. After watching Jesus teach and feed the crowd of five thousand, how do you think the disciples felt as Jesus told them to get into the boat? (14:22)

3. Where does Jesus go after He dismissed the crowd? (14:3) Why do you think this may have been so important to Jesus?

4. What are the disciples doing while Jesus is praying? (14:24) What problems are these experienced sailors facing?

5. Have you had times in ministry where everything fell apart? What doubts did you experience?

6. What does Jesus do to help His struggling disciples? (14:25) How does the storm affect Him?

7. When has Jesus helped you through the problems in your ministry and life?

8. What does Peter ask of the Lord? (14:28) What do Peter's actions reveal about his personality?

9. Why does Peter begin to sink after a few steps? (14:30) What lesson is there in Peter's failure for us?

10. Jesus reaches out to save Peter (14:31) What does that say about our Lord in our times of failure?

11. Jesus asks Peter why he doubted. (14:31) What are the situations that cause you to question your Lord? Why should you rely on Jesus in difficult times?

24
Forsaken for You
Matt. 27:32-50

Crucifixion was not new. Many in the ancient world including the Assyrians, Persians, and Greeks used it long before Jesus was put on the cross. It was such a severe form of execution that it was illegal for a Roman citizen like St. Paul to be crucified for their crimes. This horrible method of death became the symbol of Christianity after Constantine the Great was converted in 313 AD. History records that he saw a flaming cross in the heavens and God promised that "By this sign, you will conquer" before a great battle.

Having faced six trials through the night and early morning and been beaten by Jew and Roman alike, Jesus is expected to carry his cross. He cannot do it, and a stranger is enlisted for the task. The Romans took His clothes, and the Jews stood before the cross and ridiculed Him. Only one of His disciples dared to come to the cross (John 19:25-27), and the women watched from a distance (verses 55-56). In His last hours, Jesus received minimal comfort or support. He was forsaken by friend and foe as He took our cross and saved the world.

1. What do you think would be the worst way to die? Would you want to die slowly or quickly? Would you want to die alone or in the midst of your friends? How do you think crucifixion rates among the ways to die?

2. Who is forced to carry Jesus' cross? (27:32) Why does Jesus need this help?

3. Having nailed Jesus to a cross, what do the soldiers do with his possessions? (27:35-36)

4. What do you think it was like being hung naked in a public place for hours? How does that deepen your appreciation of what Jesus did for us?

5. What was the official charge against Jesus? (27:37) In what way was it true?

6. What three groups taunt Jesus? (27:38-42) What do you think is the motivation for each group?

7. When have you or someone you care about been mocked? Why does it hurt so much?

8. The chief priests call on Jesus to save himself. (27:42) What would have happened if Jesus had saved Himself?

9. What does Jesus cry out in verse 46? What does it show about the depth of Jesus' isolation?

10. What significance is there to the fact that the temple curtain was torn in two? (27:51) Why do you think the earth shook and people rose from the dead? (27:52)

11. How would you explain the necessity of Jesus' death to a nonbeliever? What feelings does the cross illicit in your life?

27
Darkness Turns to Joy
Matt 28:1-10

The resurrection of Jesus from the dead is the one truth that unites all Christians. Without the resurrection of Christ, there would be no Christian Church. Our Lord's resurrection has conquered sin and given all who believe salvation. We know that we will rise from the dead on the last day and be taken to heaven. The resurrection also assures us that Jesus has returned to heaven and that He is now ruling the world for the benefit of His people. The resurrection is the hope of God's people and the certainty of all that we believe. It is no wonder that all four gospels tell this message and what it means for all of us.

Early Easter morning, the women who had remained at the cross (Matt. 27:55-56) came bringing spices to finish the burial of Jesus. They had no thought of the resurrection and were not even sure how they would move the stone blocking the tomb's entrance (Mark 16:3). Their darkness would soon turn to joy. The story of Easter is the light in the life of every Christian. It separates those who only know about Jesus from those who believe in Him. It is the center of the Christian faith and the touch point of God's love for us.

1. If you could go back in time and visit any historical event, which event would you choose?

2. Who visits the tomb? (28:1) Why did they feel it was necessary to come?

3. What emotions do you think the women had that morning as they walked to the tomb? How would you have felt if you were in the group?

4. What events had happened at the tomb before the women had come that morning? (28:2-4)

5. What news did the angel tell the women? (28:5)

6. How did you come to know that Jesus had arisen? What convinced you that the account of His resurrection was reliable?

7. What command did the angel give the women (28:7) which Jesus repeats to them (28:10)?

8. Who is Jesus telling you to go and describe the news of the empty tomb?

9. How does Jesus show love for the women and His disciples (28:9-10)

10. Why is the resurrection so important to the Christian faith?

11. How do the words of Jesus comfort and challenge you? What stands out to you in this account of the resurrection?

29
Paul's Conversion
Acts 9: 1-19

No person, other than Jesus, dominates the pages of the New Testament more than Paul. Paul wrote thirteen books of the Bible. More than half the book of Acts follows the ministry of Paul. He is often thought of as the thirteenth disciple of Jesus, and his theology shapes our understanding of what it means to be a Christian. He began as a persecutor of the church and was turned by God into a man who would sacrifice all so that others might have salvation. His influence would span across the Roman world from Damascus to Spain. Even now, we owe much of who we are to Paul.

The story in Acts 9 records Paul's conversion as he traveled to Damascus only three years after the resurrection. There he was confronted by the risen Christ and brought face to face with the gospel message of salvation. The encounter with Jesus shaped Paul's life and destiny. Paul would refer to his conversion in Acts 22 before his arrest in Jerusalem and before King Agrippa in Acts 26. It was the start of a relationship with God that Paul would pass on to generations of Christians through his writings.

1. Who was the bully that everyone feared in school when you grew up?

2. Some of the Christians had fled Jerusalem and traveled to Damascus. What was Saul's plan and why do you think it was so important to capture these Christians? (9:1-2)

3. Describe what happened in verses 3-8 from the viewpoint of a companion of Paul on the road.

4. How did God first get your attention either to become a Christian or to take His call more seriously?

5. How does Paul react to the vision he has been given? What feelings do you think that Paul had during the days he sat in Damascus?

6. When have you found yourself confused about your relationship with the Lord? How did the Lord help you through that time? What did you learn about God or yourself?

7 Who is Ananias and what does the Lord call Ananias to do? (9:11-12) How does he respond? (9:13-14)

8. When have you obeyed the Lord like Ananias even when the task seemed dangerous or foolish?

9. How does the Lord describe Saul to Ananias? (9:15) What is to be Saul's fate before the Lord? (9:16)

10. What does Ananias call Saul (9:17) and what do you think that meant to Saul?

11. Who do you know that seems out of God's reach and will never come to faith? What does this lesson challenge those assumptions?

Leader's Guide

02
Abraham Tested
Gen. 22:1-19

Abraham had many choices to make. His story begins with a decision to set out with his family for a strange land because of a promise from the Lord. All he had, in the beginning, was the incredible promises of God (Gen. 12). In the gift of Isaac, those promises had a face and future. Now, 40 years later, God calls Abraham to make a choice even more demanding than the first. It was a decision that required that he believed that God could keep those promises even if Isaac died.

God sent Abraham to the land of Moriah which is probably modern day Jerusalem, about 50 miles from where he was living. He would arrive on the third day which gave Abraham a lot of time to turn back or change his mind. This chapter records the greatest test that Abraham ever faced. I am sure that Abraham and Isaac came down the hill different men. Abraham becomes the man of God who trusts the Lord and becomes the model for the Jews in years to come. Isaac becomes the faithful patriarch who trusts the Lord with only one failure mentioned in the bible (Gen. 26). This test that seems so shocking taught them both the mercy and love of God.

1. What possession would be hardest for you to give up?
Answers will vary. Let the group share their most prized possession. Let them discuss why that object is so valuable. It may be something that they use everyday or something that reminds them of an occasion or person. Our goal is to help them see how hard it was for Abraham to give up the most important person in his life.

2. What command does God give to Abraham in verse 2? What is at stake for Abraham if Isaac dies?
God came to him with a command that no one wants to hear. "Take your son, your only son, Isaac.. sacrifice him there as a burnt-offering" (v.2) It was a test to see how much Abraham loved his God. Abraham was being asked to sacrifice the greatest thing that God had given him because he trusted the Lord. Abraham had waited for 25 years for this son. He knew that all the promises of God depended on Isaac. If Isaac was gone, there would be no descendants as numerous as the stars and no one to inherit the land. Surely, Isaac's life was more precious to Abraham than his own life.

3. How does Abraham respond to this command? (v.3)
Trials can be used to teach us to obey and follow God's commands. "Early the next morning Abraham got up and saddled his donkey" (v.3) If God is to teach us, we must be in the right place. Abraham could have refused to take the journey, and the lesson would never have happened. Instead, he makes a painful journey to Moriah as the Lord commands. It was at Moriah where the lesson was to take place. We often think that we have a right to demand that God should solve our problems and help us with our needs on our schedule. Only when we have obeyed the Lord and are at His place and time will we find the real solutions.

4. What do you picture Abraham thinking as he hears and responds to this command? Why do you think that Abraham

did not object to God's command?

Answers will vary but might include fear, doubts about God's love, and anger. It was an unreasonable request. Isaac had been a gift to Abraham and Sarah at an age when children seemed out of the question. Abraham's future is wrapped up in this child. You have to believe that Abraham knew that God always fulfills His promises and that somehow God would keep the promises of Genesis 12 and the promises about Isaac in a way that Abraham could not see. He did not want to lose the Lord even more than he did not want to lose his son.

5. How would you feel if you were asked you to make a big sacrifice for your ministry?

Answers will vary, but encourage the group to voice their concerns and their pain in making those decisions. Often we want to know "Why me?" and seek another way. In my ministry, I had an opportunity to serve at a new church, but it would have meant leaving my adult children behind. In the end, I couldn't do it. I felt that I needed to be near my kids and continue the work I was doing here.

6. How far away is Moriah (v.4)? How would this make the test more difficult?

God didn't ask Abraham to take his son and sacrifice him immediately. It would have been easier to strike Isaac down quickly while you had your nerve. Abraham was called to make a long journey to the sacred mountain. It was "on the third day Abraham looked up and saw the place in the distance." (v.4) The three-day journey gave Abraham plenty of time to turn back and refuse what seemed to be a cruel request. Here, there would be no wife or servants to stop him from completing the task. Here he would have to fight only his desires as he sacrificed his precious son.

7. Many think that Isaac is a teenager at the time of the test. What question does he ask (v.7) and how does Abraham

answer (v.8)?
Isaac asks where the lamb is for the burnt offering. Abraham replies that God will provide the burnt offering. Remember that Abraham could not have offered Isaac without Isaac's consent and cooperation. Isaac, as the bearer of the wood, is the stronger of the two. As a young man, he is also faster than his father. Isaac is strong enough and big enough to resist or subdue Abraham. In a way, this is a question of his obedience, too.

8. On the mountain, how does Abraham show the depth of his faith? (v.10) Do you think that Abraham would have killed his son?
In the end, he was willing to give back to the Lord the greatest gift that he had received. "Then he reached out his hand and took the knife to slay his son." (v.10) He believed in the promises of God so much that he trusted that God would give his son back to him somehow. What God would do with the sacrifice, Abraham did not know. He could only trust God and know that his God had always loved him and would keep the promises He had made about Isaac. There may be people in the group who do not believe that Abraham would have killed his son. Don't argue with them, just ask them why they feel the way that they do. Such a strong faith is often hard to understand.

9. When does God stop the sacrifice (v.11) and what can we learn from God's timing?
God chooses the time. Only at the last minute does the Lord provide for His servant. The lesson has had its full effect. God could have stopped Abraham after one day of the journey or even at the foot of the mountain. It was only when the lesson was complete that the Lord provided an answer. He wanted Abraham to know and act as if he believed that the Lord would provide the lamb for the burnt offering. God will not allow us to quit in the middle of His trials but wants us to

grow fully from experience.

10. How does God provide the sacrifice as Abraham said he would (v.13)?

When the time and place are right, God often provides an ordinary answer. God could have sent an angel down from heaven with a lamb or miraculously made one appear before Abraham. God often does things in a way that seem ordinary. In this case, He just allowed a ram to get caught in a bush by its horns. Some would call it a coincidence. It was so unobtrusive. We know that it was God's way of providing. Abraham needed an animal for the altar that he had built and God arranged for him to have one at the very moment that he needed it. God often uses the ordinary things of life to provide help at just the right time.

11. What does Abraham's example teach us about trusting the Lord enough to obey Him in every situation?

Answers may vary, but include the power of faith and the love and mercy of God. Life can be tough, but God can handle anything that the world throws at us. We just have to wait for His time and His solutions. If we stop trusting because God takes too long, we can keep the blessing and answer of God from coming.

03
Joseph Reveals Himself
Gen. 45:1-28

The story of Joseph is the story of God taking a selfish man and developing a patriarch who would save his people. Along the way, he was betrayed and deserted by his family, exposed to sexual temptation, punished for doing the right thing, imprisoned, and forgotten by those he helped. As Joseph took each step, he grew into the leader that God was calling him to be. His attitudes were transformed, and people began to see the hand of God in him. Finally, he was ready to be the leader that God envisioned.

In Genesis 25, we see how completely Joseph had changed as he greets his brothers after many years. While they expected punishment for their crimes against him, he embraces them and weeps at the reunion with his family. He understands that God had sent him ahead to preserve the family. Joseph tells his brothers, "You intended to harm me, but God intended it all for good. He brought me to this position so I could save the lives of many people" (Genesis 50:20). The brother who had boasted to others about dreams had exchanged his dreams for the dreams God had for his family and the future.

1. What are family reunions or holidays like with your family? Is there someone that has been missing that you would like to see?

Answers will vary. Let the group focus on the joys and discomfort that families gathering can bring. If someone has a story that they want to share, let them do so. Make sure that you limit the stories so that the lesson can continue.

2. Judah has just offered his life for the life of Benjamin to save his father Jacob tremendous pain (Gen. 44:18-34). How does this show of mercy affect Joseph? (45:1-2)

Joseph's brothers had sold him into slavery because of their jealousy over Jacob's greater love for Joseph than his love for them. Judah knows that Benjamin is loved more by their father than any of the rest of his sons. Instead of being jealous once again, he is willing to sacrifice his own life for the family. The great change in his brothers and their willingness to put others first causes Joseph to cry intensely. He sends the Egyptians out of the room so that he can reveal himself to his brothers in private. The meeting was a family matter, and he did not want others to witness the reaction of his brothers or see his heartfelt expression of love.

3. When Joseph reveals himself to his brothers, what is their response? (45:3) What would it take for you to believe that someone was a lost relative who you thought was long dead?

The simple statement "I am Joseph" exploded like thunder in their ears and brought terror to their hearts. Confusion and memories must have cascaded through their minds. Was it really their brother? As the details of the past rolled off the lips of this stranger, fear began to grab hold of them. If it truly is Joseph, what punishment will he inflict on them for their past treatment of him? They were totally under his control, and they were speechless as they stood before him and felt judged for their sins. Two things should have stood out for them. Egyptians did not come close to Hebrews (Gen. 43:32), but Joseph asked them to come near. He wanted to be near them. Second, Joseph wept uncontrollably and with deep passion. These were not the actions of one who wanted to hurt them.

It would also be hard for us to believe that someone was a lost relative. We might require proof either in stories that they can share or the witness of someone that you believe.

4. How did God transform the evil that they had done into a blessing for the family (45:4-7)

Remind the class of the story of Joseph. He was here in Egypt because his brothers had sold him into slavery (37:12f), but God had used this wicked act to provide for the family. The family is only in year two of a seven-year famine. God will use Joseph to feed and clothe the family during the rest of the famine and beyond. His brothers were responsible for Joseph's suffering, but God had used the incident to humble a proud Joseph and provide for the future of Abraham's family.

5. How does God sometimes help us by allowing us to go through adverse circumstances?

Joseph's story reminds us that God is still in charge. We need to trust Him with our life and our future. We can't control the future, but we know that God has the power and the wisdom to bring blessings to His people. Don't forget that Joseph was, in many ways, also responsible for his slavery. He was a proud boy who consistently taunted his brothers with dreams of his superiority to his family and with boasts of his father's love. God used the slavery and other adversities to transform a proud young man into a servant of God.

6. What are Josephs' plans for his family? (45:9-13) Who does Joseph want to see?

Since Joseph is a powerful ruler of Egypt, he sees no reason for his family to live without food in Canaan. There are five more years of famine, and there is no reason for them to continue to make trips to Egypt for food. Joseph wants them to hurry home, let Jacob know that Joseph is alive, and pack their belongings so that they can live in the fertile area of Goshen. Joseph longs to see his father. Jacob is already 130 years old (Gen. 47:9) and it has been more than twenty years since Joseph has seen his father, Jacob.

7. Has Joseph truly forgiven his brothers? What leads you to think so?
Joseph's forgiveness of his brothers is shown in many ways. He embraces them all and kisses them. He offers them all a place to live with plenty of food and land for their cattle. The sin of Joseph's slavery is not hidden but is openly discussed and Joseph shares what he believes was God's divine plan. This Joseph is radically different from the Joseph that we saw in chapter 37. The strained fellowship between brothers from twenty years ago has become intense and intimate (45:15).

8. As Joseph reveals himself, what does his message expose about the character of God?
Answers will vary but should include a discussion of God's control over even difficult situations. God's love for the family of Abraham is evident, and His control over the events of history is complete. God had a plan for His people and the young man Joseph.

9. What could you tell people about God from the story of your life? Why would that be a powerful witness?
Encourage the class to share times when the Lord helped them through a crisis or helped them to grow. Our lives are a powerful story because they are our story and demonstrate what God can do. The story of a man 3800 years ago is often not as persuasive as the story of someone who is like them and who lives in their world.

10. Compare the young Joseph who mocked his brothers (Gen 37) to the Joseph in chapter 45. What has Joseph learned at the hand of God?
Joseph has learned humility and to be the servant of his family. He is generous to his brothers giving them provisions, clothes, and silver (to Benjamin). Joseph also tells them not to quarrel along the way (45:20). There was no reason to argue about what had happened in the past. All was forgiven. The 17-year-old Joseph was never a leader in his family. The 39-year-old Joseph would be the head of this family and a nation because he was willing to be a servant to both.

11. What adversities are you facing in your life? What lessons do you think God may be trying to teach you?
Answers will vary, but encourage the class to think about how they might apply the lessons that Joseph learned in the text. Do they trust the Lord enough that they will give him the crisis in their life? Can they be generous with others because they know that God will provide for them? Are they willing to see the plan of God and His ability to use their life for the benefit of others?

07
The Lord Prepares Joshua
Josh 1:1-18

Joshua was one of only two men who left Egypt in the
Exodus and entered the Promised Land 40 years later. He
became the assistant of Moses who stood at the foot of Mount
Sinai waiting for the Ten Commandments. When Moses sent
spies to scout out the land of Canaan, Joshua was selected as
the representative of the tribe of Ephraim. He and Caleb alone
believed that the Lord could conquer this place for His people.
At Moses' death, Joshua was chosen by God to be Moses'
successor and to lead the people to conquer the land that God
promised to His people.

We find the Israelites camped east of the Jordan River
across from the Promised Land. Having mourned for Moses, it
is now time to move forward. God approaches Joshua and
calls him to lead over a million people into the land that He
promised them. While Joshua had been the assistant of Moses,
the challenge must have been overwhelming. God pledges to
be with Joshua as He was with Moses. The Lord challenges
Joshua to study and obey the scripture which Moses has left
behind. To be successful, you need to follow the Lord and
listen to what He says.

1. When have you experienced a significant change in your life?

Answers will vary but could include normal changes like going to college or getting married. Other changes might be tragic like a house fire or the loss of a loved one. If it seems appropriate, have the group share changes that were especially difficult and what they learned from the experience.

2. What is the context of our story and what does that mean for Joshua? (1:1-2)

Moses has died, and Joshua is called by God to lead the people into the Promised Land. Except for Joshua and Caleb, the older generation of Israelites which had left Egypt had perished over the last forty years. Joshua would lead perhaps a million people into a land that only he and Caleb had ever visited. Cannan was a land of walled cities and powerful armies. It was natural for him to be concerned and feel inadequate. God was commissioning Joshua to lead the people, defeat these great armies and claim the inheritance promised to Moses.

3. When have you felt overwhelmed by a task that someone gave you? How did you cope?

Most of us have felt overwhelmed by a task in ministry. It might be a building program at the church, the selection process for a new pastor, or even something simple like teaching an unruly Sunday school class. Like Joshua, we cope by relying on the promises of God and spending a lot of time in Bible study and prayer. If there is time, spend a few moments on such a story of one of the group or of your congregation.

4. What promise did the Lord give to Joshua (1:3-6) what conditions did God put on the promises?

Since Joshua had a threefold task to perform, God gave him a promise in each area. God would lead them across the river

Jordan and claim the land (v. 3-4). Then the people would defeat the enemy (v.5) and divide up the land according to their tribes (v.6) Each of the promises is unconditional since God has chosen Joshua to be the tool to accomplish God's unconditional promises to Abraham (Gen. 12). Notice that God does not give Joshua a detailed plan of how God will accomplish these things. Joshua is required to trust the Lord and know that the Lord will give directions as they are needed.

5. What promises has God given you for your ministry?
The Bible is filled with messages that the Lord has given us. Three of my favorites are: "The Lord is my shepherd, I shall not want" (Psalm 23:1), "Trust in the Lord with all your heart… and He will make your paths straight" (Prov. 3:5-6) and "Surely, I am with you always, to the very end of the age." (Matt. 28:20) Encourage the group to share some of their favorite promises and how they have been helpful in their ministry and life.

6. Why was it important for Joshua to be "strong and courageous"? (1:6)
Before God could fulfill the promises that He had given, Joshua had to exercise faith. If did not move forward trusting the Lord, the people would not follow. God would call him to do some miraculous and unorthodox things like sending the ark into a flooded Jordan so that the river parted (3:8) and to march around Jericho for seven days (6:3-4). Joshua had to trust the Lord and obey the Lord completely. If he doubted what the Lord was asking or hesitated because the enemy seemed large or the people were afraid, the mission would be in danger. He must be the presence of God for the people, and His faith would inspire them to have faith.

7. What commands does God give Joshua in verses 6-9?
In addition to the command to be strong (v.6), God gave the

tools for building Joshua's faith. He was to receive
encouragement and power from the written word that Moses
had left behind (v.7) Moses had left the first five books of the
Bible as a legacy of what the Lord had promised to His people
and of the story of how the Lord had continued to be with His
people. Joshua was to read these words again and again so
that they became a part of his being. He to memorize these
words so that He could recite them and let them guide him
through the most difficult times.

**8. How courageous do you feel in ministry right now? How
does your courage in ministry or lack of courage affect your
fellow servants?**
The question is not meant to accuse the group or make them
feel guilty, but to honestly examine their feelings. We often
feel that our ministry is between God and us, yet we see in the
text how God makes it clear that Joshua's ministry will affect
the faith of the nation. Have the group look at the effects of a
faithful and faithless leader on the ministry. Pray for a leader
at your church if you feel that he or she is keeping you from
reaching your God-ordained task.

**9. Why is meditating on God's word so important for Joshua
if he is to be courageous? Why does it matter to you?**
Answers will vary, but we all need to know that we will not
be able to accomplish the ministry we have been given or to
live with real peace and success without the Lord. The
blessings of life come by following God's path and the Bible is
where we learn what that path is and where we learn the
values and morals that will guide us in life. We don't have the
power to overcome our private demons or our personal crisis,
but God can handle all of them. He empowers us through His
word and gives us an advantage that nothing else can match.

**10. How does Joshua show that he believes the promises
that God has made? (1:10)**
Joshua immediately conveys God's plan to the leaders. He

doesn't ask for their advice, but as their commander begins the preparations that are needed for the nation to obey the Lord (v.11). Joshua also exudes faith and confidence. He tells them that "you will cross the Jordan, " and you will "take possession of the land" (v.11) He is acting as the confident and courageous leader that the Lord was commanding him to be.

11. How do the people respond to Joshua? (1:16)

The leaders of the twelve tribes catch the enthusiasm and faith of Joshua. They recognized that Joshua spoke for God and gave him a pledge of complete obedience. Their commitment and faith would pass on to the people that they commanded. The nation would live by faith and not repeat the failure of their parents 40 years ago. Their reaction must have been a blessing to Joshua. It encouraged him to take over Moses' position of leadership and move forward with God's plan.

12. What challenge lies before you right now? What do you need to do so God can prepare you for success?

If the group is part of one church, talk about the challenges that your church faces. Be honest about the challenges, but also realize that God is bigger than every crisis that we might face. Review how the courageous faith of Joshua inspired the whole nation. What can this group do to be such an inspiration to the congregation or each other?

09
Ruth Meets Boaz
Ruth 2:1-23

A woman from the pagan nation of Moab, Ruth became the mother of Obed and great-grandmother of King David. Her story set during the time of the Judges reminds us that God wants to change our hearts so that He can change our circumstances. God is not here to make us comfortable. He desires to change us from the inside so that we can have the attitudes and values of His people. Ruth who begins outside the nation of Israel shows true loyalty to the Lord that is missing throughout much of the time of the Judges. It is her character and her faith that allows the Lord to remake her life and choose her to be one of the ancestors of Jesus.

The Book of Ruth tells the story of a Jewish family that leaves Israel during a time of a famine and has life go from bad to worse. All three men in the family die leaving Naomi and Ruth in a desperate situation. Returning to Judah, it is Ruth who leads the family back into God's promises by her willingness to work and to trust the Lord. She will marry Boaz and become part of God's chosen people. No one is outside God's grace and mercy if they will but trust in Him.

1. Have you ever lived or worked on a farm? What was your fondest memory?

I worked on a horseradish farm in southern Illinois for three summers. The work was hard, but I was fit and trim by the end of the season. Encourage others to tell their stories. If no one has worked on a farm, perhaps there are stories of a family garden.

2. How does Ruth provide for herself and Naomi (2:2) What dangers might she face by working there?

Ruth does not seem like a woman who could remain idle. She asks Naomi's permission to glean in the fields so that the two of them could have food to eat. It was part of God's law that the Jews were to allow the poor glean to feed themselves. It was God's program of welfare. Being a stranger, Ruth did not know who owned the various pieces of land. She was also a woman and an outsider and was vulnerable to attack.

3. If you suddenly had no means of supporting yourself, how would you react? What can we learn from Ruth about being calm and taking advantage of opportunities?

Too often I have panicked and caused myself more trouble than I was already facing. Our tendency is to look at what we can do. Even if we are calm and logical, our plans often do not include God. Ruth trusted God and looked for the opportunities that were available to her. God had commanded that farmers were to leave gleanings for the poor. Have the group discussed how they have reacted to difficulty and what they admire about Ruth's actions.

4. Who is Boaz and what kind of man do you think he was? (2:4-5)

Boaz is a relative of Elimelech, Naomi's husband, and seems to be an important man in the city (Ruth 4). He is the owner of the fields and shows respect to Ruth. He provides for her and has his men protect her while she is working in the fields. He is flattered (Ruth 3: 10) when she approaches him for redemption and is honest in his dealings with her and with the nearest relative to Elimelech (Ruth 4:4)

5. How Did Boaz's foreman describe Ruth (2:6-7)

After sharing Ruth's connection to Naomi, the foreman describes Ruth's humility as she asked for permission to work in their fields. He also expresses how hard she works. Other than a short time in the shelter, Ruth has worked steadily throughout the day so that she can provide as much as she can for Naomi and herself.

6. What character traits of Ruth stand out to you? How would those qualities give an advantage to any Christian?

Allow the class to think of traits that they see throughout the book of Ruth. They might mention her loyalty to Naomi, her humility or hard work in the fields, or her willingness to seek opportunities instead of being bitter like Naomi seems to be at the end of chapter one. The advantage such Godly traits would give to anyone would be obvious. They open Ruth and us up to let the Lord provide more opportunities for us and bring us up out of the valleys of life.

7. What specific instructions did Boaz give to Ruth, and how did she respond to him? (2:8-11) How do they each show respect for the other?

Ruth would never have spoken to Boaz. He was a landowner and leader of the city. She was an alien widow who was a stranger. It is noteworthy that Boaz interrupted his conversation with the foreman to go and speak to Ruth. He called her "daughter" and promised to treat her as if she was part of the family. She was not to leave his fields but to integrate herself among the young women. He promised to protect her and gave her the right to drink from the water jugs of his workers. He would also feed her (v.14) at mealtime. His words show tremendous respect for her. She bows down before him and acknowledges the enormity of his kindness wondering what she has done to deserve such gracious treatment.

8. What reason did Boaz give Ruth for his particular attention to her? (2:11-12)

Boaz recognizes all that Ruth is doing for Naomi and all that she has given up. She is hardworking, faithful to her mother in law and brave when she is presented with unfamiliar opportunities. Ruth could have been bitter like her mother in law (1:20). Instead, she has chosen to come to this foreign land and embrace the Jewish God as her own. Ruth has gained a reputation for consistently showing this character in her life. Boaz's prayer is that the Lord reward her and care for Ruth because of the choices that she has made.

9. How did God show His faithfulness to Ruth and Naomi?

While Naomi was bitter against God because of the hardship she had experienced, Ruth was open to God's help. God began with Ruth and through her brought healing and aid to Naomi. Ruth's story started with the death of a husband but would end with the birth of a child who would be the ancestor of our Savior. Have the class explore the many ways in this story that the Lord worked to achieve a new future for Ruth and Naomi. Let them find instances of God's hand in making the events unfold to bring about the ending of the story.

10. How did Naomi respond to Ruth's success (2:19-20) How does Ruth's success changer Naomi's view of the future from when she first arrived in Judea? (1:20)

The abundance of Ruth's gleanings surprised Naomi. An ephah of grain was about 3/5 of a bushel and was enough to feed them for a week. She immediately wanted to know what had been the source of such blessings. She was overjoyed when she found out that it was Boaz who had shown Ruth kindness. This joy is in stark contrast to the bitterness that she had shown in chapter one. She blesses the Lord here while she was bitter to the Lord in chapter one.

11. Judging from the events in this story, what character traits does God honor in His people? How does your life reflect these character traits?

Answers will vary but might include faith in the Lord or the willingness to use the opportunities given. Someone in the class might also mention Ruth's humility, hard work, and respect for the kindness of Boaz. Let the class explore these character traits and their impact on our lives. Ask the class which qualities they would see as most beneficial for their lives.

12. How have you opened yourself to God's miracles in your life?

This question asks how they have used the opportunities that the Lord has given. The same opportunities were available for Naomi as were for Ruth, yet only Ruth saw the opportunities. We can be bitter like Naomi or trusting like Ruth. The choice is ours. Take time discussing with the group ways that they shut their life off from the Lord. Do they listen to His guidance in the Bible? Do they ignore lessons from Bible study or messages in worship? We have to hear and obey what the Lord is telling us if we are to gain the advantages that Ruth received.

11
David Spares Saul
1 Sam 24:1-22

David was the youngest of eight brothers in the city of Bethlehem. He was the keeper of his father's sheep and is well known for the many psalms that are attributed to him. David would rise to fame for killing the giant Goliath and soon was a general for Saul, the first king of the united Israel. He soon fell out of favor as Saul became jealous of David and his success. He would spend years as a fugitive before Saul's death in battle elevated David to succeed him as king.

The story in this text happens during the days when David was a fugitive being pursued by Saul. He and his men were hiding in a large cave in Southern Israel to escape Saul's pursuit. Saul enters the cave alone to relieve himself, and David faces the temptation to end the pursuit by killing Saul. His actions that day showed the character of David to Saul and David's men. It showed why the Lord had chosen David to succeed Saul and lead the people of God as King.

1. How does it feel when you suddenly have a rival or enemy at your mercy? What are you tempted to do?
Answers will vary. Our temptation is to use the opportunity to get even. Someone has hurt us, and we want to mistreat them or even the score. We may even feel that the Lord has given us this opportunity.

2. What is the setting for our story and why has Saul come to this remote area? (24:1-2)
David has been hiding safely in a region called Engedi, an oasis on the western side of the Dead Sea. Saul has not been able to find him, and David and his men have been safe and secure. Saul decides to gather a force of 3000 men to go and track David down. He wants David and has ignored his enemies the Philistines to go and pursue David. Just when it looks bad for David, something amazing happens. It is a trial of a different type that will test David and strengthen his faith.

3. Why did Saul enter the cave where David and his men were hidden? (9:3) What did David's men think God was doing? (9:4)
The Law of Moses required each soldier to leave the camp to relieve himself meaning that Saul was away from his men and very vulnerable. Since he walked right into the cave out of dozens that David was hiding in shows the hand of God in this story. David's men see the hand of God in Saul's actions, too. David is hiding in this cave with some of his 600 men. Every one of David's men present must have thought that this was a God-given opportunity. David should kill Saul so David and his men would no longer have to run like hunted animals through the desert.

4. Why does David cut off part of Saul's robe? Why is his conscience bothered when he only cut a piece of cloth? (24:4-5)
David doesn't kill Saul as his men want, but he cuts a corner

of Saul's robe. It was as if he was saying I could do this and I want to do this, but I can't. Then his conscience kicks in. "What did I do?" David sees that the ugliness and anger of Saul chasing him have tempted David to be just like Saul. David thought of the promise that he had made to his friend Jonathan. David may have also thought of his men. Even taking a piece of the robe makes it look like David can take justice into his own hands. God unleashed David's conscience and taught him the lesson that this trial was all about. He was not to sink to Saul's level. David was to be better than that. He was to have the heart of God.

5. When have you found restraint speaking louder than actions? What are often the consequences of taking matters into your own hands?

Answers will vary. Encourage the group to tell a story from their lives if possible. God sometimes allows us to be in challenging situations. He will give you opportunities to get ahead of your rival. He will back you into a corner and expect you to tell the truth. It is those trials and temptations that create our character so that we can have that character when things are good.

6. When Saul left the cave, what does David do and why did he leave the cave? (24:8)

When Saul was far enough away from the cave, David left the cave and called out to him as "my lord the king" and bowed down before the king. David was showing honor to Saul and was intent on letting Saul and his men know that David was not a rebel. He respected the office of king and knew that the Lord had put Saul in that place. David wants to make it right. He will confess what he has done and treat him as the father that Saul had become to him. David will do the right thing and trust the Lord to protect him.

7. Why is it not enough to just confess our sin to the Lord?

Why do we need to admit what we have done to the person that we hurt?

Answers will vary but just saying you are sorry to God is not enough. You have to make it right. You have to go and confess to those you have hurt. We have to go and admit that we are to blame for a failed project. We have to clean up the mess that we have made in someone else's life. It is not just enough to admit to God that you are wrong.

8. What proof did David give concerning his character? (24:11) What does David call on the Lord to do for him? (24:12,15)

Lifting up the piece of Saul's robe, David asserts his innocence. David had a chance to kill Saul and did not do so even though many of his men wanted David to do just that. Saul should not listen to people who say that David is his enemy. David calls upon the Lord to judge which of them has the right character and which of them is evil. It would be easy to see these words as a big "God is going to get you." I think that David is trying to get Saul to focus on God and to obey God before it is too late. David seems to care about Saul.

9. How does Saul respond to David's words? (24:16-21) What does he know and what request does he make of David?

Even the unjust often know that God will care for his own. Saul himself confirms that David will one day be king. God uses the words of Saul to strengthen David's faith and admit that no one can change the will of God. God's ways will triumph and will bring blessing for His people. There may also be a measure of fear in Saul's voice. Both Saul and Jonathan fear David's anger and fear that David will not stay righteous, but will kill all of Saul's family when David become king. He asks David to swear that he will show kindness when he becomes king.

10. As you think about how the story plays out in the next

couple of chapters, what is the difference between Saul and David? How have you seen the Godly triumph and the wicked defeated?

Answers will vary. I am sure that God would have liked to make both men the Godly king that could lead Israel. Any man can stop God from making them a saint. Saul seems to make a full confession here and appears to accept the lesson that the Lord has taught him. He is a broken man who will soon be back hunting David and ignoring what he has just learned from the Lord. David would keep this promise. He would not kill the members of Saul's house. He would take over the kingdom only after Saul and his sons had fallen in battle.

11 As you look at this story, how does God used trials and tests to shape His people?

Answers will vary. God will use trials like this to shape his people. Those who listen to the Lord and learn his lessons will find that blessings will follow as they are shaped by God's character in their lives. Those who ignore the lessons will find that they will sow the seeds of their destruction. You may not always enjoy the trials that the Lord gives you, but you will always benefit.

13
Solomon Asks for Wisdom
1 Kings 3:1-15

His annual income was 25 tons of gold a year, and riches were all around him. He sat on an ivory throne overlaid with gold, received tribute from kings and merchants and drank from goblets made of gold. He was so rich that silver had almost no value in the days of Solomon. The queen of Sheba came like many others to see if the rumors were true and found that his wisdom and riches exceeded every tale. She declared that those who lived in the kingdom of Solomon were incredibly blessed to live in such a kingdom of riches, peace, and wisdom.

When Solomon ascended the throne, the people of Israel soon learned that he was not another David. He was a scholar, not a soldier, a man more interested in erecting buildings than fighting battles. This passage is the story of the opportunity that God gave to Solomon to be as great a ruler as his father, David. He chooses wisely in this story, but there are already hints of the women that would weaken his resolve for the Lord. Solomon would live in luxury with treaties with many nations even as Solomon would realize that wisdom and wealth were not enough to bring happiness. (Eccl. 12:13-14)

1. If a genie gave you a single wish, what choice would you make?
Answers will vary. Most of us remember the story of Aladdin and the magical lamp. Encourage the members of your group to tell their wish. You might even pass a lamp or other object for them to rub and make their request. The question helps us to understand the opportunity that Solomon had and the wisdom that he showed at this point in his life.

2. David had conquered the nations on the battlefield. Solomon chose diplomacy by marrying the daughters of foreign kings. What country is first to give their princess to Solomon (3:1) and what is the outcome of the marriage? (3:3)
His first bride after he became king was the daughter of the Pharaoh of Egypt. She and other wives would cause Solomon to worship at other places than the tabernacle and temple. It was the beginning of the lust that took Solomon away from God. He filled his life with women – 700 wives and 300 concubines from the nations that he conquered. (1 Kings 11:4) He permitted these women to worship their gods instead of insisting that they worship the Lord. Then he began to worship their gods with them. He demoted God to being one God among many by loving these women more than he loved the true God.

3. Where does Solomon go early in his ministry and how does he show where his heart is at this point in his life? (3:4)
Solomon goes to Gibeon, a town located about five miles north of Jerusalem, where the tabernacle is located. He has gathered all the leaders of the people of Israel (2 Chronicles 1:1-6) so that they may offer a sacrifice of a thousand burnt offerings on the altar there. It would be an offering uniting the people before God and showing the love that the young Solomon had for the Lord. It was an assembly that probably lasted all day as Solomon and the people remained at Gibeon for the night even though Jerusalem was not far away.

4. What did God say to Solomon? (3:5) How is this not only an incredible opportunity for Solomon but also a test of Solomon's heart and character?

The Bible mentions both Nathan and Gad as counselors for David but names no prophet in Solomon's circle of advisers. We see God speaking to Solomon here and in chapter 9. God says "Ask for whatever you want me to give you." That is a fantastic offer, but it is also a test of Solomon's heart since people usually ask for the things for their pleasure. His request of wisdom may come because of his age. Many commentaries put Solomon in his early 20's when he ascends the throne. He has a temple to build and a powerful kingdom to rule.

5. What is Solomon's petition and how does he preface his request? (3:6-9)

Solomon humbly looks back and acknowledges the kindness and love that God had shown to David. Solomon also honors the Lord for choosing him to be the king after his father. He contrasts the kingdom's greatness with the fact that he is a little child. Based on God's goodness and his desire to rule well, Solomon asks for the wisdom to make the most of the opportunities that the Lord might bring. Solomon wants a heart that will discern what God's will is so that he might follow the Lord and serve the people well.

6. Because God was pleased with Solomon's request, what other gifts did God give Solomon? (3:10-13)

God was pleased with Solomon's request for wisdom for it showed his concern for the people and for obeying the Lord. He gave him wisdom that was so great that there would never be anyone like him. He also gave him the riches and honor that he did not request. We can see the depth of that wisdom that Solomon wrote in the book of Proverbs. We can also get a sense of the honor that people gave Solomon in the account of the Queen of Sheba (2 Chronicles 9).

7. What conditional promise does God make with Solomon? (3:14) Why was obedience so essential for the continuation of the blessings that the Lord was giving Solomon?
The promise of long life is contingent on Solomon walking in God's ways and obeying God's commandments. He knew the covenant that the Lord had made with the people in Deuteronomy and the covenant that God had made with David (2 Sam. 7). Obedience was not a new concept for Solomon. If he were to enjoy the wealth and wisdom that the Lord was giving him, he would need to live in obedience to the Lord. Sadly, Solomon forgot the Lord and drifted away from the Lord. God would chasten him and split the kingdom in two as a result of Solomon's sin.

8. After Solomon had built and dedicated the temple, God would come to him with another promise in 1 Kings 9:4-7. What are God's promise and God's warning for Solomon?
God offered Solomon a legacy. He would see a dynasty of his descendants on the throne. Everything that God said to David would belong to him. God was promising to make this a nation where the countries of the world might come to Israel and learn about Him. Centuries of good times could be ahead. There was a condition, and that condition was obedience. Solomon needed to be a man like his father who led the people to follow their God and live with His values. Only a Godly nation could become the beacon that God had in mind for Israel. Sadly the curse of verse 7 came to pass. God cut off Israel and rejected the temple that Solomon had built.

9. Unfortunately, the wisest man that the world has ever had did not keep the promise to obey the Lord all his life. Why is obedience such a key to enjoying all the blessings that the Lord has given? (Eccl. 2:10-11)
"Meaningless, meaningless, all is meaningless," said Solomon.

He had wealth, power, and wisdom; but it meant nothing. He pursued one pleasure after another, but it only left him empty. Such was life without God. It was a life of having everything, but it was all a waste. If the life of Solomon teaches us anything, it is that forgetting God makes life meaningless. Real joy comes in having a relationship with God and in the knowledge that you and I have a heavenly Father who will keep on giving. We don't know what tomorrow will bring or if we can handle it. God not only knows the future but will protect and provide for those who love Him.

10. What interests are close to your heart? Is there a decision that you are facing now that needs the wisdom that only God can give?
Answers will vary. It is important to look at this story and see what God is willing to give to His people when they have His will in their heart. Churches and individual Christians can do amazing things if they have the heart for serving God and serving others. God will provide the things that we need to change the world. Dream big for your God can do amazing things if we will

18
Daniel in the Lion's Den
Daniel 6:1-28

His ministry would span from the time he was taken by Nebuchadnezzar as a teenager in 605 BC until the first year of Cyrus in 536 BC. He and his three friends were examples of faith to generations that struggled with a lack of faith. Their devotion to the Lord brought them to the highest levels of foreign governments and gave them opportunities to witness to kings and nations how exceptional the real God was. Daniel was a man of honesty and prayer. Foreigners recognized Daniel's character and praised the true God because of what they saw in Daniel and learned from him.

At the time of this text, Daniel was over 80 years old and had become one of top three administrators in the nation. He attracted the attention of King Darius because of his honesty and ethics leading Darius to desire to put Daniel above all the other leaders. A trap is set for Daniel, but Daniel will not give up the worship of His God to save himself. His trust in the Lord gives God the opportunity to show the world that He is the true God. It also shows His great love for His prophet near the end of Daniel's life.

1. Under what conditions would you consider stepping into a lion's cage?

The only safe answer might be when they were newborn kittens. I saw a lion playing with a three-foot diameter ball at the Cleveland Zoo a couple of years ago and was amazed at how he batted that thing around like it was nothing. It was fun to watch, but I was glad that I was outside the glass.

2. Why did Daniel's colleague's plot against him? (6:3-4) How did they plan to discredit Daniel? (6:5)

It would seem that Darius may have suspected that some of the officials that he inherited were not honest. Since he needed an honest set of eyes over everything, he elevated a semi-retired Daniel to be one of the three key administrators over the kingdom. This promotion alarmed the other officials who knew of Daniel's reputation and feared that they would not be able to use their offices for personal gain. Since they could not discredit Daniel because of his honesty, they decided to set a trap because of his faithfulness to the Lord. If they could make it illegal to pray to the true God, then Daniel would be caught.

3. How did Daniel respond to the king's decree? (6:9-10) What motivated Daniel to respond that way?

Daniel continues his prayer life before the Lord as if the decree doesn't exist. Verse 10 tells us that he knew about the proclamation and began to pray immediately. It was like any other problem in his life. He would bring it to the Lord and let the Lord deal with the problem. Darius began reigning in about 539 BC making Daniel about 82 years old at the time of this edict. Encourage the class to speculate what was going through Daniel's mind. My guess is that he had grown in his faith and seen how the Lord had blessed him. He was not going to lose the Lord this late in life.

4. What would Daniel have lost if he had given up praying to the Lord for the 30 days of the edict?

Answers will vary. I think that many of us would have prayed privately during the 30 days. Daniel prayed in public because he did not fear death and he trusted the Lord to deal with those who put him in this position. He did not want to lose the close relationship that he had with the Lord. I also think that the Jews in Persia must have looked to Daniel for spiritual leadership. If he hid his faith, many of them would have had their faiths impacted. His public prayer in spite of the decree was a witness to the Lord that should not be lost.

5. Where is your faith challenged in life? What is at stake if you overcome the challenge or give in to trials to your faith?
Answers will vary. Our faith can be challenged at work or in some of the groups to which we belong. Our temptation is to stay quiet, but that does a disservice to God and others around us. How will people know the truth if God's people don't lovingly tell the truth or live out their character and values? How will others around us become bold to live their faith out if everyone just gives in to the world? Don't let the world tell you to give up on God. How can we expect God to help if we are outside His values?

6. Why is the king so distressed (6:14) What is the king's hope for Daniel? (6:16)
The king seems distressed because he had foolishly given into pride and been manipulated by the men he did not trust. He was about to lose the one man who could help him govern the empire. Had Darius taken the time to talk to Daniel or others about this edict, he might have discovered the real motive of the officials. He tried to find a way to save Daniel but failed. The officials came to Darius and reminded him of his duty (6:15) and leaving him no choice. His only option was to utter a prayer that God would miraculously save Daniel. Having no hope of his own, Darius was forced to rely on the true God.

7. What happened during the night? (6:18-22)

The king could not sleep. He refused food and would not be entertained. He spent a sleepless night and even fasted. One imagines that he spent the whole night thinking of Daniel. Daniel, on the other hand, was unharmed. In the darkness, he was safe because the Lord shut the mouths of the lions and kept him safe. He may have even slept while God's angel kept the lions at bay. The presence of the angel would have given him confidence in the Lord.

8. Why doesn't God save every Christian who is persecuted?
Answers will vary. It would be pleasant if every Christian could count on God saving them from every persecution. It is often through hardship that God teaches His people and shows the world His strength. God, in His wisdom, knows whether the death or life of His saints will bring the most people to faith. I think of Shadrach, Meshach, and Abednego who told King Nebuchadnezzar that God could save them, but if He didn't, they still would not worship the king" Gods. (Daniel 3:16-18) Christians need to obey the Lord and trust Him to choose the outcome.

9. Why do you think God saved Daniel? (6:23) How did God's deliverance of Daniel affect the king?
Surely part of the reason for Daniel's deliverance is that it witnessed to the king and everyone in Persia that the Lord was truly God. The miracle taught Darius that the Lord was a living God and not a dead idol. Darius' weak faith (Is your God able to deliver you?) becomes a public expression to all the people of God's power and deliverance. God could have kept Daniel from ever being in the lion's den, but the rescue brought greater honor to God among both Jew and Persian. Imagine how the news of Daniel's deliverance would have spread throughout the city and the country. Everyone would have been in awe of what God had done.

10. What happened to Daniel's accusers and their families?

(6:24) Why do you think the King punished them?
The traitors were judged and thrown into the lion's den with their families. As if to show the extent of Daniel's miracle, the lion's overpowered the traitors before they hit the floor. It was probably their punishment for conspiring to trick the king and for forcing him to follow the edict (v.15). Families were included so that none of them could scheme to kill the king in revenge. The action made all others who might oppose the king think twice about their actions.

11. When have you experienced trials for your faith? How has God helped you through those times of trial and trouble?
Answers will vary. Encourage the group to tell their stories and any lessons that they may have learned. Also, ask how their actions may have influenced others just as Daniel's faith influenced the king and others.

20
Mordecai Persuades Esther
Esther 4:1-17

The story of Esther begins in 483 about 100 years after the Fall of Jerusalem and 50 years after the first group of Jews has returned to Jerusalem. The Persians are in power and Judea is just a vassal state miles away from the palace where our story will occur. It is important to realize how powerless the Jews are at this point. Whatever the Persian king says is law, and it must be obeyed. While God is never mentioned directly in the book, there is no doubt that God is working to save His people. Esther becomes queen in an unlikely series of events, and God uses her words and actions to overturn an evil plot against his people.

What is this plot? The new prime minister has a long-time grudge against the Jewish people and has paid the king for the right of exterminating the Jews. Jews all over the kingdom are wailing and wearing sackcloth. Since the Persian Empire stretches from India to Ethiopia, there are few places for the people to run. Jews all over the kingdom are concerned about the race being wiped off the earth. Esther is the story of how God can change the world if one person is willing to take a risk.

1. When have you taken a risk and had it work out better than you thought it would?
Answers will vary. Let people tell their story. Ask them what the consequences would have been if things had not worked out.

2. In Esther 3:13, an edict from the king was made. What was the edict that is the background for all of chapter 4?
The prime minister of the Persians hates the Jews and has paid a hefty sum to the king to have an edict proclaimed that all the Jews in the kingdom are to be slaughtered. The nation will be wiped out in all the lands of Persia (including the Jews back in Jerusalem). This crime will happen on one day, and all the possessions of the Jews will be confiscated. The extent of this action cannot be underestimated. Jesus will not be born nor will people like Ezra, Nehemiah or Malachi have their ministries.

3. How do Mordecai and the other Jews react to the news? (4:1-4)
They cried out as if someone died for they knew that death was their fate. There was no reason to hide their grief for they wanted the whole world to know the injustice that was being done. Mordecai took his mourning to the gate of the palace. The officers at the gate already knew that he was a Jew; now Mordecai was telling the whole city that he was not only a Jew but also that a great evil being done to the Jews. As you read the story, it would seem that Esther may not have known about the edict before Mordecai's actions. She seems insulated inside the palace from such news.

4. How have you reacted to an injustice to you or to Christians who are persecuted because of their faith?
Answers will vary. Encourage the group to share any stories or to be honest about how they might have reacted in Mordecai's place. I have noticed some protesting or having

prayer vigils to enlist God's help. Most, however, have kept silent about our faith. Far too few hear about the love and good choices that God gives in the Bible. The world continues to act foolishly because no one tells them the truth.

5. Mordecai refused to be appeased by new clothes from Esther. His refusal of clothes caught her attention. What was Mordecai's message and what did Mordecai ask Esther to do? (4:6-9)
When Mordecai refused the gift of new clothes, it was a signal to Esther that something was drastically wrong. She could not go and see Mordecai but sent one of her eunuchs to find out what was happening. Mordecai laid out all the facts of the decree and even had a copy of the edict for Esther to read. He does more than just inform the queen; he calls upon her to share her Jewish ancestry and intercede for her people. One wonders what Hathach, the eunuch, felt when he found out that Esther was Jewish.

6. How does Esther reply to Mordecai? (4:11) Do you think she was denying Mordecai's request or is it something else?
I think her response is not a denial, but an explanation and her own request. The plan to exterminate the Jews was news to her. She is looking for direction at what she can do. I think that isolated in the harem; she was looking for some guidance from a man she trusted who also seemed to know more about the workings of Persian government than she does. She knows the king she is married to is not a nice man. He also thinks so little of her that he has not sent for her in a month. Had she already fallen out of favor? He has already gotten rid of one wife and could easily get rid of her. Her doubts are getting her, and she seeks help knowing what to do.

7. How does Mordecai respond to Esther's message? (4:12-14)
Mordecai's response seems a little harsh. He appears to think that she wants to hide her nationality. I wonder if he

misinterpreted Esther's message. Remember they could not
speak to each other, but had to communicate through an
intermediary. In his response, Mordecai reminds Esther that
ignoring the evil will not make it go away. People will find
out that Esther is a Jew and destroy her as well. No place is
safe. He ends with the argument that God may have put her in
this position for a reason. Others like Joseph had been situated
in places of honor to save the people of Israel.

8. What is the problem with just ignoring evil?
Answers will vary. The group needs to wrestle with the fact
that ignoring evil today will not make it go away. When we
ignore evil, people think that we are in favor of it. We allow all
the people who don't know any better to believe that they are
making wise choices when they commit adultery or think of
all religions as foolish or as being the same. We would do well
to share our faith with our friends so that they understand
what the Lord teaches and why we think that is a better way.
Otherwise, we will continue to live in a broken society that
assumes it has all the answers.

**9. How does Mordecai show that he believes that God will
deal with the problem no matter what Esther does? (4:14)
What does this say about God's control of the future?**
Mordecai trusts God and believes that God will not allow His
people to be destroyed. I wonder if Mordecai is thinking of all
the promises that God made to Abraham (Gen. 12:2-3). He
firmly believes that the Lord will defeat this evil bent on
destroying the Jews. God has a plan, and Mordecai believes
that Esther can be a part of that plan. If she refuses to help,
then God will need to raise up another person and save the
nation in another way. It all comes down to God being the
Lord of everything. Nothing is outside His control. Evil may
raise its head, but God will control the future and protect His
people.

10. What is Esther's request so that she can prepare to see the king? (4:15-16)

Esther doesn't just barge into the king's room expecting that God will protect her and make everything work out. She will fast and pray for three days, and she asks that all of the Jewish people fast and pray with her. She wants to do this by God's power and not on her own. I picture her pleading to God for his plan for the salvation of her people. I imagine her bowing before her God and offering herself as His tool. She knows the power of those who are plotting evil. She also knows the power of her God and will not go forward without him.

11. In what kind of situations would it be good for Christians to fast and pray?

Answers will vary. There may be situations that the group members want to share. My observation is that our tendency is to act quickly and decisively. We have the two-minute prayer before a church meeting and then hash out what we think is the right solution. I have found that the Christian church fails because it doesn't spend enough time in prayer. Evil in our world is powerful. Only those who spend time praying to the Lord privately or in groups for hours at a time will know what the Lord wants them to do.

23
Jesus Walks on Water
Matthew 14:22-34

The Gospel writers recorded only a fraction of the miracles that Jesus did. He raised the dead, healed the sick, cast out the demon, and showed his power over nature. There was nothing that He could not do. Often, His heart was touched by the pain of those who were suffering. He would stop what he was doing just to help those in need. His miracles were proof that He was from God and drew people to come and listen to the message that He shared.

The Gospel of John tells us why Jesus sent His disciples away after the feeding of the five thousand. Jesus knew that the people wanted to make Him king and He did not want the disciples to fall under the desires of the crowd. On the water, they faced a storm and learned of the Lord's concern for them and the depth of His power. Peter reaches out to the Lord so that he can experience God's power and not just see it. He begins to sink when he takes his eyes off Jesus. This miracle can teach us to lean on Jesus through the storms of our lives.

1. What is the scariest experience that you have ever faced?
Answers will vary. Let the group members tell their own
stories and how the situation worked out for them.

**2. After watching Jesus teach and feed the crowd of five
thousand, how do you think the disciples felt as Jesus told
them to get into the boat? (14:22)**
It was about a year into Jesus' ministry, and things were going
very well. The crowds were coming, even hounding Jesus.
John tells us that the people wanted to make Jesus king after
the feeding of the 5000. It was a time when there seemed to be
nothing that Jesus couldn't do. He could heal any illness, and
His messages amazed the people. I picture the disciples on a
great high convinced that the ministry of Jesus could not fail.
Everything would be simple to a master that had this kind of
power.

**3. Where does Jesus go after He dismissed the crowd? (14:3)
Why do you think this may have been so important to Jesus?**
After he dismisses the crowd, Jesus goes up on a
mountainside to pray. Jesus knew that the masses wanted to
make Him king by force (John 6:15). That may have been more
of a temptation that we think. It is similar to Satan's
temptation to give Jesus all the kingdoms of the world. (Matt.
4:8-9) Here on the mountainside He could be with the Father
and renew His strength. Jesus could focus on the task that the
Father had given Him and leave the distractions behind.

**4. What are the disciples doing while Jesus is praying?
(14:24) What problems are these experienced sailors facing?**
Jesus must have told them to get into the boat around sunset.
The text finds the disciples still rowing to get across the sea
rowing at the fourth watch – about 3 AM. It is dark, and what
should have been a simple journey has been the boat ride
from hell. Some of these men are experienced fishermen who
have fished all their lives on this lake and been in many

storms, but they are afraid. In the boat, they began to doubt Jesus. Just at the time of greatest triumph (so far), things fall apart, and the disciples find themselves on the Sea of Galilee with the waves getting choppy and the wind blowing them around.

5. Have you had times in ministry where everything fell apart? What doubts did you experience?

Answers will vary. Have the group tell their stories and share their fears. It is nice to know that we are not the only one who has struggled. Our struggle is that if we believe in an all-powerful God, we think ministry will be easy. Sometimes the hardest challenges are right after our greatest times of success. As we pat ourselves on the back for a job well done, tragedy strikes, and we find ourselves struggling and wondering what went wrong. Like the disciples, we do everything we can think of to stay afloat.

6. What does Jesus do to help His struggling disciples? (14:25) How does the storm affect Him?

Having had his time with the Father, Jesus is untouched by the storm. Mark 6:48 records that Jesus saw the disciples straining at the oars. Mark's gospel also tells us that Jesus seemed like he was going to walk by them and meet them on the other side. Only when they are terrified at what they must have assumed was the grim reaper come to take them away, did Jesus speak. He reached out to calm them and stop them from focusing on themselves and focus instead on Him.

7. When has Jesus helped you through the problems in your ministry and life?

Answers will vary. Let the group tell their stories. The point is that God is bigger and stronger than the great problems that can overwhelm us. What can our trials or troubles do to Him? He has confidence in His plan for us and is never as worried about things as we are since he can handle them all. Seeing our terror and hearing our prayers, He speaks to us as well assuring us of His ability to handle all the things that can harm us. He wants us to have the same confidence that He has for the future.

8. What does Peter ask of the Lord? (14:28) What do Peter's actions reveal about his personality?

Peter asks to come to the Lord on the water. One wonders if Peter senses that it is safer out on the water with Jesus than in the boat. Peter has the faith to see that Jesus can do what he cannot. He realizes that Jesus can bring those clinging to him safely to the other side and he wants to be with Jesus. Peter is impetuous throughout the scripture. He boldly tells everyone that he will not deny his Lord on the night before Jesus dies. Here, Peter shows faith. In the boat he is relying on his own abilities, out on the water, he will rely on Jesus.

9. Why does Peter begin to sink after a few steps? (14:30) What lesson is there in Peter's failure for us?

Peter began to look again at the storm all around him. Perhaps a wave rolled over his feet, or the wind began to howl. He began to wonder what would happen if Jesus couldn't hold him up. He began to wonder if he wouldn't have been safer in the boat. At the moment that he stopped trusting, the miracle ceased and Peter began to sink. It was not the miracle that failed. It was Peter who stopped believing and started looking again at himself. Even as miracles happen for us, the storm will still be all around us. And the moment that we stop trusting him, we will begin to sink.

10. Jesus reaches out to save Peter (14:31) What does that say about our Lord in our times of failure?

When Peter fails; the Lord is still there for him. Immediately the text says Jesus reached out his hand and caught his disciple. Jesus would not let him drown. Peter in his fear cried out once more to the Lord, and the Lord reached out and helped him. There will be times when we fall as well. We are human and will start thinking of the waves around us. Those are the times when all seems hopeless to cry out in prayer to the Lord. He will be there for us and will save us if we think of him again and call.

11. Jesus asks Peter why he doubted. (14:31) What are the situations that cause you to question your Lord? Why should you rely on Jesus in difficult times?
Answers will vary. I can still hear Jesus's voice asking me, "Why did you doubt?" on more than one occasion. We will all avoid a lot of grief and pain if we can continue to trust in him and rely on his ability to make the miracles happen. His power will not fail even when the seas are rough, and the storm howls. It is a comfort to know that He will take us by the hand and lead us to safety as well. Jesus is the Lord who listens to the cries of His people and helps them to achieve the goals that He has for us. As He steps into the boat with us, the storm is gone as well. He calms it just by His presence.

24
Forsaken for You
Matt. 27:32-50

Crucifixion was not new. Many in the ancient world including the Assyrians, Persians, and Greeks used it long before Jesus was put on the cross. It was such a severe form of execution that it was illegal for a Roman citizen like St. Paul to be crucified for their crimes. This horrible method of death became the symbol of Christianity after Constantine the Great was converted in 313 AD. History records that he saw a flaming cross in the heavens and God promised that "By this sign, you will conquer" before a great battle.

Having faced six trials through the night and early morning and been beaten by Jew and Roman alike, Jesus is expected to carry his cross. He cannot do it, and a stranger is enlisted for the task. The Romans took His clothes, and the Jews stood before the cross and ridiculed Him. Only one of His disciples dared to come to the cross (John 19:25-27), and the women watched from a distance (verses 55-56). In His last hours, Jesus received minimal comfort or support. He was forsaken by friend and foe as He took our cross and saved the world.

1. What do you think would be the worst way to die? Would you want to die slowly or quickly? Would you want to die alone or in the midst of your friends? How do you think crucifixion rates among the ways to die?

Answers will vary but focus on the horror of death and how it can be made even more horrible. Crucifixion was one of the worst ways to die. It could take days, was very public and humiliating, and was extremely painful. The bible spends very little time describing the horror of crucifixion, but it surely was terrible.

2. Who is forced to carry Jesus' cross? (27:32) Why does Jesus need this help?

His name is Simon, and he was from Cyrene in North Africa. The gospel of Mark (Mark 15:21) adds that he was "the father of Alexander and Rufus." Since the gospel of Mark was going to the Romans and Paul mentions a Rufus (Romans 16:13), it may be that Simon's actions of carrying the cross led to his conversion to the faith. If you consider the beating that Jesus took at the hands of the Jews (Matthew 26:67) and again from the Romans (Matt. 27:27-31), it is easy to see why Jesus was in no shape to carry the heavy cross.

3. Having nailed Jesus to a cross, what do the soldiers do with his possessions? (27:35-36)

Contrary to the modest artwork we are used to seeing, Jesus would hang virtually naked. The Romans considered His garments part of their spoil and divided them between the soldiers. They even gambled over the choicest piece (John 19:23).

4. What do you think it was like being hung naked in a public place for hours? How does that deepen your appreciation of what Jesus did for us?

Living in a nation where even the worst criminals have rights, we struggle to understand the humiliation that Roman crucifixion was meant to be. Each criminal hung on a cross to slowly and painfully die. It was an advertisement for the people that they should not oppose the Roman government. The extent of the pain and the humiliation of the cross were meant to deter crime. Once the Romans found you guilty, you had very few civil rights.

5. What was the official charge against Jesus? (27:37) In what way was it true?

The official charge (which the Jews had brought against Jesus in Luke 23:2) was that of being a king. John 19:20 tells us that the charge was written in three languages so that anyone coming to Jerusalem could read the charge. The Jews felt Pilate was mocking them and protested the sign (John 19:21). If this stripped and executed man was truly the king of the Jews as the Jewish leaders had claimed, His execution would be seen as an insult every Jew. The truth of the sign was simple. As Messiah, Jesus was the king of His people. He was dying for them that they might have freedom and the opportunity to be children of God.

6. What three groups taunt Jesus? (27:38-42) What do you think is the motivation for each group?

Jesus will be mocked by the two robbers on either side of Him (27:38, 44), the crowd passing by (27:39) and the Jewish leaders (27:41-43). Let the class put themselves in the shoes of each group and find the motive they would have had in their place. One suggestion would be that the robbers mocked Him because here was the only one that they considered in a worse situation than they were. The crowd passing by got caught up in the spirit of things and mocked Him for fun. The Jewish leaders certainly mocked Jesus out of hate. They had Jesus where they wanted Him and were enjoying the opportunity to pay Him back for the trouble that He had been.

7. When have you or someone you care about been mocked?

Why does it hurt so much?
Let the class relate their stories. Mocking by itself seems to do
no physical harm but causes deep scars emotionally as it
changes how we see ourselves and changes the relationships
that all of us need to survive. We often think that it was easy
for Jesus on the cross because He was God, yet He was also a
man and would have felt the loneliness and the insults very
deeply.

8. The chief priests call on Jesus to save himself. (27:42)
What would have happened if Jesus had saved Himself?
Jesus had saved many during His ministry including raising
people like Jairus' daughter and Lazarus from the dead. The
Jewish leaders taunt Him to save Himself (27:42). Could He
have saved Himself? Surely He could have. Jesus had
explained to Pilate that His servants would have fought to
rescue Him if His kingdom were of this world (John 18:38). It
is hard to believe that He could not have called down for a
legion of angels if He had truly wanted to be free. To save
Himself would have meant to doom us. Someone has to pay
for sin, and Jesus offered Himself freely so that we might have
salvation.

9. What does Jesus cry out in verse 46? What does it show
about the depth of Jesus' isolation?
Jesus' cry of My God, My God, why have you forsaken me?"
is not one of despair but is a quote from Psalm 22:1. The psalm
speaks of the isolation as God is "so far from saving me," but
quickly turns to the fact that God is enthroned as the Holy
One (Psalm 22:3) who delivered those who trusted in Him
(Psalm 22:4). Jesus knew that God would not be able to look
upon His Son the moment that Jesus took our sin upon
Himself, but that the victory of the resurrection was the
deliverance for those who trusted in the Father. Thus those
words echo the pain of the cross and the hope of salvation for
those who trust in the Lord.

10. What significance is there to the fact that the temple curtain was torn in two? (27:51) Why do you think the earth shook and people rose from the dead? (27:52)
The temple building consists of the Holy Place where only priests could enter and the Most Holy Place where the High Priest could enter once a year to place blood for atonement. The curtain separating these two areas was torn at Christ's death showing that the barrier between God and humanity was removed. We are now free to approach God as His children. The darkness (27:45), the earthquake, and the dead appearing in town reminds us that the death of Jesus could not go unnoticed by the people of Jerusalem. Everyone present would know that this was not an ordinary death whether they believed in Jesus or not.

11. How would you explain the necessity of Jesus' death to a nonbeliever? What feelings does the cross illicit in your life?
The cost of the cross was great, but Jesus' death was the only way to our salvation. Let the class focus on the sacrifice that Jesus made for us and the love that drove Him to our cross. Challenge the members of the class to explain the benefits of the cross to them and to the non-Christians that they know. Don't let this be an exercise in guilt, but a celebration of the love Jesus has for us. We should feel honored and loved because our Savior would do this for us so much that we would share it with others.

27
Darkness Turns to Joy
Matt 28:1-10

The resurrection of Jesus from the dead is the one truth
that unites all Christians. Without the resurrection of Christ,
there would be no Christian Church. Our Lord's resurrection
has conquered sin and given all who believe salvation. We
know that we will rise from the dead on the last day and be
taken to heaven. The resurrection also assures us that Jesus
has returned to heaven and that He is now ruling the world
for the benefit of His people. The resurrection is the hope of
God's people and the certainty of all that we believe. It is no
wonder that all four gospels tell this message and what it
means for all of us.

Early Easter morning, the women who had remained at
the cross (Matt. 27:55-56) came bringing spices to finish the
burial of Jesus. They had no thought of the resurrection and
were not even sure how they would move the stone blocking
the tomb's entrance (Mark 16:3). Their darkness would soon
turn to joy. The story of Easter is the light in the life of every
Christian. It separates those who only know about Jesus from
those who believe in Him. It is the center of the Christian faith
and the touch point of God's love for us.

1. If you could go back in time and visit any historical event, which event would you choose?
Each person will have their own choice. Easter morning would be high on my list. Let the people make their own decisions first. Then ask what it would be like to have hidden in the bushes and watch Easter unfold. The point of the question is to put yourself in the story.

2. Who visits the tomb? (28:1) Why did they feel it was necessary to come?
Mary Magdalene and the other Mary came at dawn. Both of them had been at the cross (Matt. 27:56) and followed Joseph so that they would know where the tomb was located (Matt. 27:61). The women came early in the morning after the Sabbath because they had not had any time to prepare the body before the Sabbath began at sunset on Friday. (Mark 16:1) It was common to use perfumes on the body since the Jews did not embalm the bodies. This visit was their time to say goodbye to Jesus.

3. What emotions do you think the women had that morning as they walked to the tomb? How would you have felt if you were in the group?
Have the group put themselves in the place of the women. The women came to the tomb to finish the job of embalming a friend that they were sure was dead. Common answers might include crying, shock, and a sense of helplessness or loss. Let them answer about their feelings. The women have the feeling that one of us might have visiting a grave a day or two after the burial of a close relative or friend to place flowers on the grave.

4. What events had happened at the tomb before the women had come that morning? (28:2-4)
The Lord had prepared the tomb for the visitors by a violent earthquake and a visit by an angel which scared the guards so

that the women had an unimpeded visit at the grave. The
description of the angel provides ample reason for the guards
to be afraid. The angel also rolled the stone away so that the
women could see into the tomb and be witnesses to Jesus'
resurrection. God knew that a closed tomb guarded by
soldiers would not have allowed the women to see that Jesus
was gone or hear the witness of the angel. The events of the
morning prepared the tomb for the discovery of the
resurrection.

5. What news did the angel tell the women? (28:5)

The angel reassures the women that they have no reason to
fear. They are looking for Jesus, but He has risen. The angel
reminds the women that Jesus had told them three times
(Matt. 16:21, 17:22-23, and 20:17-19) that He would rise. They
should not have been surprised because Jesus had prepared
them for this moment. Each of the three predictions in
Matthew's gospel gives more details than the prediction
before it. The angel also invites the women to look into the
tomb and see the place where Jesus had been laid. John's
gospel (John 20:6-7) even describes the grave clothes to show
that no one could have made off with the body.

6. How did you come to know that Jesus had arisen? What convinced you that the account of His resurrection was reliable?

Many of us have been Christians since our childhood and thus
have just accepted the resurrection as truth. Others in the
group may have come to faith as an adult. Let the group share
why they believe in the resurrection. Some may believe
because of a miracle that happened in their lives. Others may
accept the resurrection because the story has convinced them.
Some may not be sure why they believe. Accept their ideas
and let the group discuss what convinces people that Jesus is
alive so that they can share that witness with others.

7. What command did the angel give the women (28:7) which Jesus repeats to them (28:10)?

The angel commands the women to proclaim what they have seen to the disciples in verse 7. Jesus will repeat this command in verse 10. Remember that the disciples were gathered (Luke 24:9) and were probably experiencing the same fear and sadness that the women had felt as they went to the tomb. God's concern for His servants is evident. He wants the disciples to have the good news as soon as possible. Sadly, the men did not believe the women's testimony (Luke 24:11) because the resurrection of Jesus seemed like nonsense.

8. Who is Jesus telling you to go and describe the news of the empty tomb?

Answers will vary, but have the group think about people that they know who are struggling or who have questions about life. God gives us all opportunities to let the message of the gospel help the hurting around us. We have the good news just as the women did that first Easter. Our task is to go and tell others so that people around us might have the joy that we experience. It is true that many are satisfied in life and are not very open to the message. That should not stop us from sharing our faith. Each person should make a list of the hurting who the Holy Spirit can prepare to listen and believe our message.

9. How does Jesus show love for the women and His disciples (28:9-10)

Jesus could have just let the angel present the message, but in His love for them, He appeared directly to them as they hurried away from the tomb. His words assure them that He harbors no anger to them or to the disciples who He calls "brothers." His greeting is one of closeness and love for them. He also gives instructions for the disciples to go to Galilee even though He will see them in Jerusalem later that day (Luke 24:36). The disciples who deserted Jesus in the Garden of Gethsemane and at the cross are forgiven and restored. Jesus will not abandon them.

10. Why is the resurrection so important to the Christian faith?

Answers will vary. Let the class wrestle with why Easter is so important. For me, it is the heart of faith. Because Jesus rose, I will rise again, and that changes the future of every Christian. The resurrection helps me when close friends and family die. I know that I will see other Christians again in heaven. The resurrection reminds me that Jesus is ruling the earth and that He can do anything that I ask Him and that He will give me whatever I need. Easter affects my past by wiping away my sin, my present by giving me a Lord I can call on at any time, and my future because it means that I will get to live in heaven with Jesus and others.

11. How do the words of Jesus comfort and challenge you? What stands out to you in this account of the resurrection?

Answers will vary and may include the lengths that God went to so that people might know that Jesus rose or the love of Jesus shown to the women and disciples who did not believe in Him at first. I think of the joy that they had that day of actually seeing Jesus and the women's reaction of falling at His feet and worshipping Him (as God?).

29
Paul's Conversion
Acts 9: 1-19

No person, other than Jesus, dominates the pages of the New Testament more than Paul. Paul wrote thirteen books of the Bible. More than half the book of Acts follows the ministry of Paul. He is often thought of as the thirteenth disciple of Jesus, and his theology shapes our understanding of what it means to be a Christian. He began as a persecutor of the church and was turned by God into a man who would sacrifice all so that others might have salvation. His influence would span across the Roman world from Damascus to Spain. Even now, we owe much of who we are to Paul.

The story in Acts 9 records Paul's conversion as he traveled to Damascus only three years after the resurrection. There he was confronted by the risen Christ and brought face to face with the gospel message of salvation. The encounter with Jesus shaped Paul's life and destiny. Paul would refer to his conversion in Acts 22 before his arrest in Jerusalem and before King Agrippa in Acts 26. It was the start of a relationship with God that Paul would pass on to generations of Christians through his writings.

1. Who was the bully that everyone feared in school when you grew up?

Answers will vary. In the text, Saul comes across as someone that you don't want to cross. The discussion of bullies may be a good way to get a handle on Saul, the zealot who thought he was doing God a service by persecuting the church. He was bold and brash and sure that he was right.

2. Some of the Christians had fled Jerusalem and traveled to Damascus. What was Saul's plan and why do you think it was so important to capture these Christians? (9:1-2)

Saul was first mentioned at the stoning of Stephen (7:58) and here seems so zealous for the Jewish faith that he begins to persecute all who believed in Jesus (followers of the Way). He requests letters from the High Priest both to introduce himself to the local Jews and give him the authorization to seize Christians and drag them back to Jerusalem. It may be that the Jews feared the spread of Christianity and the trouble that this new sect might cause for the Jews of Jerusalem.

3. Describe what happened in verses 3-8 from the viewpoint of a companion of Paul on the road.

The men who were with Paul were probably happy to be traveling with someone who had been given the authority of the High Priest. Suddenly as they were near Damascus (9:3), a bright light shined on the group. They all fell to the ground afraid. Saul saw someone up in the sky and talked to Him, but the others saw nothing (9:7). They heard the words telling Saul that it was Jesus and that Saul was to go into the city for further instructions. The bold and courageous man who was their leader a moment ago was now blind and confused. As he lay on the ground, Paul was broken.

4. How did God first get your attention either to become a Christian or to take His call more seriously?

Answers will vary. Many of us have had a moment that

brought us closer to the Lord. Let the members of your group discuss that moment. For some who were baptized as children like I was, there often is a time when we took a significant leap in our walk of faith. Let those who have been Christians all their lives discuss that time. It may have been a tragedy like a death in the family. It may have been a mission trip or other service event. God can use both good and bad events to help us grow.

5. How does Paul react to the vision he has been given? What feelings do you think that Paul had during the days he sat in Damascus?
Paul had seen the bright light and heard the voice telling him that the light was from Jesus who Saul was persecuting. Saul was seeing the Shekinah light or the glory of God that shown at the temple. The light connected to the voice telling him that the crucified Jesus had been resurrected by God and exalted in glory. Saul was not serving God when he persecuted the Christians. He was opposing God himself. The days Saul sat in Damascus were days of confusion and terror. He had felt so right in all that he had done, but he had gotten it all wrong. In one instance, Saul was humbled and overwhelmed.

6. When have you found yourself confused about your relationship with the Lord? How did the Lord help you through that time? What did you learn about God or yourself?
Answers will vary. Most of us had times when we were angry at God or confused about our role in His kingdom. It may have been a family member that died and made us angry, or it may have been a ministry that failed, and we were seeking answers about why disaster came. We can get upset with God, or we can do as Paul did spending our time praying and being in the word. Let the group share any of their experiences. It is important for us to look at what the Lord was trying to teach us by the experience. Hardship is often the best teacher.

7. Who is Ananias and what does the Lord call Ananias to do? (9:11-12) How does he respond? (9:13-14)

Paul later describes Ananias as "a devout observer of the law and highly respected by all the Jews living there." (Acts 22:12) The Lord sends this converted Jew to go to see Saul at the house of Judas on Straight Street and restore Saul's sight. The Lord has prepared a praying Saul for this visit and for the message that Ananias will deliver to Saul. Ananias first responds to the Lord with a willing heart (9:10) as others like Abraham, Jacob and Samuel have. Once he hears the task he has been given, he is more than a little concerned. The persecution by Saul was well known, and Christians wanted to stay away from him.

8. When have you obeyed the Lord like Ananias even when the task seemed dangerous or foolish?

Most of us in ministry have had calls to people we didn't want to make or tasks that we did not want to do. Let the group tell their stories and share any good things that happened because of trusting the Lord. Sometimes people do repent if a caring heart reaches out to them. Sometimes miracles do happen when we take on something that everyone else believed could not be done. As we share our stories, we see the power of God in action.

9. How does the Lord describe Saul to Ananias? (9:15) What is to be Saul's fate before the Lord? (9:16)

Saul is God's chosen instrument. The Christian hater from Tarsus had been chosen by God to be the vessel to bring the gospel to the Gentiles. Saul's task for the rest of his life would be to bring the gospel to the world. As we look at the remainder of the book of Acts, we can see the suffering that this task caused Saul as he was beaten and imprisoned and eventually martyred for the message. God had prepared Saul for this responsibility by training this Jew at the feet of

Gamaliel and giving him citizenship in the Roman Empire so he could travel the empire freely.

10. What does Ananias call Saul (9:17) and what do you think that meant to Saul?

Ananias calls Saul brother. The man who had been persecuting Jesus and the church had received a blessing from Jesus and been accepted into the Christian church as one of them. Saul received his physical sight but also received the Holy Spirit so that he could see the truth about Jesus and witness to his Lord. The visit gave encouragement to a troubled Saul and a vision of what the Lord wanted him to become. This message must have been a day he felt the burden come off his shoulders and a new life begin.

11. Who do you know that seems out of God's reach and will never come to faith? What does this lesson challenge those assumptions?

Answers will vary. I know that I am guilty of writing off people who I think are beyond salvation or growth. It might be nice to close the session by praying for those people by name. Let the group name friends and relatives who seem too far gone for them to help. Pray for those people and ask the Lord to open up their eyes as He did Saul's eyes. The lesson for us all is that God can turn the heart of anyone and use them in His kingdom.

Simple Bible timeline

Abraham	2166-1991 BC
Exodus	1446 BC
Entrance into Canaan	1406 BC
Judges	1375-1050 BC
Saul's reign	1050-1010 BC
David's reign	1010-970 BC
Solomon's reign	970-930 BC
Fall of Samaria	722 BC
Fall of Jerusalem	586 BC
Daniel	605-536 BC
1st exiles return	538 BC
Esther becomes queen	479 BC
Ezra returns	458 BC
Nehemiah returns	445 BC
Christmas	6/5 BC
Jesus ministry begins	26 AD
Easter	30 AD
Paul's 1st missionary journey	46-48 AD
Paul's execution	68 AD
Revelation written	95 AD

Other titles from Books from Higher Ground:

Wise Up to Rise Up by Rebecca Benston

A Path to Shalom by Steen Burke

From a Hole in My Life to a Life Made Whole by Janet

Kay Teresa

Overcomer by Forrest Henslee

Miracles: I Love Them by Forest Godin

32 Days with Christ's Passion by Mark Etter

The Magic Egg by Linda Phillipson

The Tin Can Gang by Chuck David

Whobert the Owl by Mya C. Benston

Add these titles to your collection today!

http://www.booksfromhigherground.tictail.com